CHI KUNG: RECLAIM YOUR POWER

An honours graduate of psychology and philosophy, Kaleghl Quinn was born in El Paso, Texas. Her international ancestral background is as multifaceted as her methods. In a remarkably short space of time she gained a second-degree black belt in Judo, learnt Kung Fu, Aikido, Tai-Chi and Chi Kung. She then integrated the academic and physical disciplines, and started to evolve and teach her well-known theory that self-defence and personal empowerment is 90 per cent attitude with 10 per cent good physical technique.

Kaleghl has taught women, men and children from all over the world, and now also teaches her methods to major international companies.

This book is dedicated to my parents, Samuel Sterling and Montie Earl, and my grandparents for providing me with the wealth of my heritage, and above all, for their abiding love and encouragement for me to be who I am meant to be, and to my sisters and brothers and all the other Earth Angels, for whom this has never been a question.

CHI KUNG: RECLAIM YOUR POWER

The Secret Art of Maximizing Your Potential

Kaleghl Quinn

Thorsons
An Imprint of HarperCollins*Publishers*

Thorsons
An Imprint of HarperCollins*Publishers*
77–85 Fulham Palace Road,
Hammersmith, London W6 8JB

Published by Mandala 1991 as *Reclaim Your Power*
Thorsons edition 1995

1   3   5   7   9   10   8   6   4   2

A catalogue record for this book
is available from the British Library

ISBN 1 85538 503 1
Typeset by Harper Phototypesetters Ltd.,
Northampton, England
Printed in Great Britain by
HarperCollinsManufacturing Glasgow

Research assistance by Joyce Halenar

CONTENTS

~

LIST OF
EARTH ANGEL STORIES

Earth Angels are living examples of the techniques described in this book. Their stories can be found on the following pages:

PREFACE

It would be more than naive to omit the importance of environmental conservation in dealing with maximizing the potential of the individual. In an ideal world, issues such as those presented by the green movement would work hand in hand with the general improvement of life quality for us all. This means that those with political authority would regard these issues as priorities on their working agendas. As it is, we cannot wait or rely upon any external authority to initiate constructive change. We become instruments of change when we embody more of our potential.

Each of us comes in with a vast sea of potential. Sometimes a bit of it is recognized in early childhood. Usually this bit of self is conditioned and cultivated within the limitations of our family and culture. Our bodies are but mere fractions of this potential. There are parts of self outside the scope of these limitations which we may access and realize if we open our minds.

INTRODUCTION

There are many apparent reasons for us to question our security in the world: inflation, the rise in crime, changes in the institutions that govern us, destruction of the earth and its natural resources – its natural inhabitants, the suffering of those of us living in poverty and other appalling conditions. And although the headlines can be overwhelming there are ways in which we, who are privileged enough to have access to the information in this book, can effect change. It begins with changes inside each of us. When we acknowledge the ways we suffer as a result of giving away our power, we open the door to our potential as helpers in the world.

Suffering is the product of holding on to anything which no longer serves us. We suffer when we forget to flow. One day, I was reading aloud to one of my classes and was surprised to see the word 'flower' divided for the first time. I was so surprised that I stopped reading and complained about it to my class. 'Why would anyone divide such a beautiful word in such a way!' I exclaimed. Flower had become flow-er. As I was describing the division to the class it suddenly dawned on me what I was reading about. The secret of the flower is that it knows how to flow gracefully with the seasons of its destiny. Equally, the secret of the flower is that it is totally what it is at each stage of its development and doesn't try to imitate other flowers or animals or humans. It simply is what it is. It has an internal knowing, a clockwork, a rhythm, with a built-in sequence of necessary experiences which guide it to its full potential. Each flower is different.

Each of us is like a flower. Contrary to the general population's conduct, the anguish that can result from trying to fit into someone else's ideas of right and wrong, someone else's reality, at the expense of trusting our own timing, the messages of our bodies, our own rhythms, and our unique response to life, is not necessary. I stand in strong opposition to this collusion and find it to be at the very root of our dislocation from all that the gift of our unique features has brought us. When 'asleep' we fritter away the gift and power of our uniqueness in comparison with others, in guilt from some religion or belief system that is limited and punitive by nature. When awake to this gift we celebrate daily and revel in our opportunities to preside as stewards of this lovely garden.

When we know when to flow, when to initiate, when to hold back, when to consolidate, and when to evaluate we become in charge of our lives. We align with our life's purpose and steer ourselves confidently through all the obstacles towards a more productive and satisfying existence. Suffering is minimized while a constructive, meaningful use of energy is maximized. Our life quality improves. This is the purpose of *Reclaim Your Power* – to provide tools for you to recognize, cultivate and develop strategies for remembering and building your power.

Secrets bear power only as long as they are truly secret. The true secrets are part of ourselves we are too shy or afraid to set free. Once revealed they make room for more seeds of their kind to bloom – to surprise us. These blossoming surprises are the vanguard to our participation in the greater flow. It is my hope that *Reclaim Your Power* will be a tool-shed for our human flowering.

The book is arranged in various sections. Although there is a logical progression of chapters, each one is self-contained and may be read out of sequence. You may open at any of them and read the chapter titles, reflect upon their meaning in sequence or on their own. You may wish to come back to some chapters months or years later. Those of you who are familiar with my work will recognize the basic thought behind the various disciplines I share. I ask only that you read each chapter with an open mind and then add your own experience.

THE EARTH ANGELS

It was no longer a secret. In many ways they were like the dynamic, yet peaceful atmosphere they emanated. Loving, radiant, warm . . . they always seemed to be in the right place at the right time. These were the people who had remembered with courage to listen to their hearts, their instinct, to treat others with kindness, to turn their ideas into action, and their dreams into reality. Mutual welfare and benefit was their salutation. Crisis equals opportunity was their motto. Because life was revered as the most potent force, they never feared the shadow of death.

So strong was their spirit that everywhere they went they inspired others with luminous integrity – an integrity that gently spread loving mists of encouragement through the layers of amnesia which kept each around them from the memory of their true destinies. They inspired others to be led by the contents of each of their heart. They moved others to stretch their minds and to cultivate elasticity.

This was not a fairy tale. No woolly-headed idealists were they. They gained their resilient strength from swimming upstream through years of confrontations, through their transmutations of personal traumas, fears of daring to be different, and social opposition – but most of all, from penetrating the void of their aloneness. These were the ones whose lives were rich with painful experiences – ones that had gracefully flowered into self-knowledge, power and compassion. These were the ones, who, before they moved into other dimensions, remembered to reclaim their power whilst on earth.

ONE AMONG THEM

What lies behind us and
What lies before us are tiny matters compared to
What lies within us

RALPH WALDO EMERSON

As a child whenever the wind would blow she would detach from her body and to into a state of trauma. For her the wind brought an image of a beautiful house in the countryside. This apparent residence was in no particular country: it could have been anywhere. When it came this image would seep through her body like a fine grey mist, then would float through her head and fill her mind with an emotional atmosphere of impending doom. How ironic was this image: a house surrounded by exquisite landscape with the promise of the warmth of home, and yet, such desolation prevailed. No one was there.

For a major part of her life it appeared that the wind was her enemy.

PART ONE

≈

The Way You Wake Up
is the Way You
Live Your Life

WAKING UP
≈

WAKE NOW OR FOREVER STAY ASLEEP!

The only real answer is to concern myself with what is uniquely me.
This gives me the impulse and the courage to act constructively on
the outside world.

ROBERT GREENLEAF

Each one of us has come to earth for a reason and there is also a reason why we look different from one another. Our unique essence is shrouded in our distinctive features. When we leave the quality of our lives to chance, luck, and other people we literally *leave* our lives. When we do this we give away our power. There are many who are unwittingly walking around dead, devoid of vibrance and a sense of purpose; aimless victims buffeted by the winds of change.

How different our lives would be if one of the first things we learned in school was, that the way we wake up in the morning can set the tone and atmosphere for the way we live and experience our day.

Although we may have lost touch with the reason why we were born through trauma, pain, lack of proper nourishment, it is never too late to reconnect with it. When we fail to participate fully in the shaping of our lives, we are among the living dead. The movement in our lives is robot-like. It lacks colour and vitality. Claiming our natural ability and right to respond to the beat of our potential is the first step to making it happen. **Remembering to listen to our**

inner voices – call it instinct, guts, intuition or music – is the vehicle to reclaiming our power.

Getting to the moon was once an impossible task. Though we admired it as the largest luminous jewel in the sky and appreciated its light, there was once a time when there was no apparent means of getting there.

We are constantly making strides in science and technology. In all our striving to push the boundaries of our limitations we seem to forget that each of us has within us the technology – the means to solving all our problems at the very least, and to fulfil our potential as easily as we breathe. Learning to take charge of our lives and channel the life-force to each of our advantages is a bit like our historic relationship with the moon. We see people around us having a good time, participating in socially uplifting activities, enjoying the rewards of their talents. Through the breath of sour grapes we call them 'the beautiful people', further elaborating: 'They always seem to be in the right places at the right times.' So admired, so envied, so despised – these *beautiful people* have often become the barometers of our individual worth. We fail to realize a means to this *joie de vivre* and persevere in miserable existences. Why?

There is definitely more to life than the malaise of existential despair. I believe behind every mystery there is a method – an orderly arrangement of ideas, tools and vehicles just waiting to be discovered, waiting to be used at any given moment. Once discovered these tools can lead us out of the catacombs of darkness into the light of understanding. Habitually used, one wakes up one morning to find the overall quality of life has improved. More opportunities are available and the world seems a friendlier place. The mystery I will be addressing in *Reclaim Your Power* is: *How to improve the feeling of our existence effectively and take it beyond the realm of survival into the heights of joyous and meaningful purpose, irrespective of one's gender, racial or economic background.*

ANOTHER AMONG THEM

WAKING UP . . . A TRUE STORY

This section begins with a story of a young man who discovered the importance of trusting his instincts.

SAM: (*On the phone*) Good morning. May I speak to the boss?

BOSS: Hello.

SAM: Oh, hello boss. I don't feel I ought to come in today, sir.

BOSS: Are you ill Sam?

SAM: Not really. I can't describe it. It's a feeling. You know I take my work seriously and I've always come in. Well, this feeling has been building inside for a while and it's really strong now. I'm thinking of resigning. Are you available to talk to me tomorrow?

BOSS: Come on Sam. What do you mean . . . you're not coming in? You don't sound ill. What's this nonsense?

SAM: It's true, as I said, I don't feel ill. It's just a strong gut feeling. I can't explain it. Somehow I just don't feel right about coming in today.

BOSS: All right Sam. Look, we've got a small job that won't even take an hour. Why don't you come in, give us a hand on this one and you can call it a day?

SAM: Something's not right. I really don't want to come in.

BOSS: Just help us out on this one and we can discuss your resignation afterwards. It'll be a cinch. You can do this one in your sleep.

SAM: (*resigned*) All right boss.

Two hours later Sam was in hospital, miraculously alive after an accident on the worksite. He was an electrical engineer, and that day became a major turning point in his life. While on the job he was struck on the back of his head at the delicate juncture of the skull and the neck at a speed of at least 100 miles an hour with 1,000 lb of pressure by a swinging metal 25-lb tool-box. The impact of the blow sent Sam flying into a chain-linked fence. Its grid design was evidence of the violent momentum as it cut its pattern a quarter of an inch into his face. As he bounced away from the fence one of his baffled mates caught his face to prevent Sam from hitting the pavement face-on. Surely, this would have been the end of him. All who knew of the severity of the accident said it was impossible for him to be alive.

Even though his eyes were closed after being hit, he was conscious throughout the entire experience. He remembered a loud K-O-N-N-N-G-G-G sound, then floating above the earth with a pleasant sensation flowing through him. It wasn't until he heard his co-workers describing the bleeding from the back of his head that he recognized that they might be talking about him. At that moment he experienced a very dense feeling as though he was being squeezed into a black lead box. He realized that he had actually died and was compelled to return to his body when he heard them talking about the blood. He told me that when he heard of the blood he used it as a sign that he was still alive rather then panicking. His strong consideration for others prompted him to request that his Mum and Dad were not told as he didn't want them to worry. Sam's obvious strong will was an important factor in his miraculous recovery. There were other dimensions of himself that he was using: superconsciousness, and the power of transmutation and humour. He described the ride in the ambulance as excruciating, the intensity of which he would have never thought possible when the vehicle hit a dip in the road. Sam's reply was: 'Damn! Where are the cadillacs when you need them?'

This wake-up experience was an initiation into other expanded awarenesses. When I asked my brother what the turning point was that caused him literally to save his own life he smiled and told me that it was a memory of something he had read in my previous book, *Stand Your Ground*. The memory invited him to translate his awareness of his red blood into the element of fire, to use it as a catalyst – as energy – to empower himself to live.

Like Sam each of us has his or her near-miss stories. There are those we can look upon as turning points in our lives, some perhaps more dramatic than others. Usually, we dismiss these events as good or bad luck. I propose that these choices have been and can be the keys which have in the past and will continue to turn our lives into gold or ashes.

How can we place the nature of these unique illusive parts of ourselves under the microscope of our individual awarenesses in order to extract meaningful information? From there, how do we proceed to uncover underlying practical laws and tools to improve the overall quality of our lives? Is it possible?

This is the purpose of *Chi Kung: Reclaim Your Power* – to encourage us to remember and claim the heritage of our *natural* power – to desegregate our private worlds from the outer reality of our lives. **In other words, we will remember to bridge the gaps between what is inside and outside.**

The manner in which we wake up every day is the key to how we live our lives. Most of us take our hellos to each day for granted. This lack of awareness keeps us veiled in the illusion that we cannot actively participate in the shaping of the feeling tone of our days. There was once a time when we took darkness for granted as the event that happens when the sun goes down. The importance of personal awareness of the way we greet our days cannot be overstated.

How do you say hello to the day? Do you find yourself flailing in anger at the tone of the alarm, forgetting that it was you who set it? Do you wake up slowly or all of a sudden? Do you wake with sadness or anxiety or joy? Or do you ignore the alarm and, in doing so, hope the day will go away?

At this time, you may wish to argue about the relevance of the simplistic and apparently naive nature of these questions. Keep reading. You'll find it is this very simplicity that allows you access to cultivate the quality of your day. Keep in mind that everything that exists is a massive multiplicity of its basic unit; just as the body is composed of cells, so weeks, months and years are products of days.

Your answers to these questions indicate the way you shape your day. It is only natural that we respond in a variety of ways. Factors such as the environment, sleeping on our own versus with another can certainly have a bearing on one's disposition. Hopefully, after working with your waking patterns you will ferret out these subtle influences and make choices as to which ones you will want to augment and which you wish to change or dissolve. Again, the purpose of this book is to remind you to retain your sense of uniqueness in all situations.

The idea behind this waking-up observation is to become aware of recurring themes. The time to start these observations is now. How did you wake up this morning? What was your mood, your disposition? If you were angry and anxious these moods will colour your day and can block sensitivity to opportunities to improve relationships, money and work problems. There are answers all around us all the time, yet we can only see them if we look through receptive lenses.

Step one in reclaiming our power lies in the awareness of how we wake up. Stripping away all the outside circumstances such as noise, temperature, the person next to you, time of day/night, etc., focus on how you open your eyes when you wake. Begin to observe the following:

1. What were you thinking about?
2. How did you feel (in your mind, your heart, your pelvis and legs)?
3. Were there any distinct physical sensations? If so, where were these sensations located in your body?
4. How did you feel towards others – in your room, in your home – that you know?
5. How did others interact with you?
6. Which obstacles did you encounter during the day?
7. Which opportunities appeared?
8. What was your response to those opportunities?

We each have our own way of observing our personal patterns.

Yours may be by jotting down notes on a writing pad on your bedside table or speaking into a tape recorder, or reflecting on your waking later in the day, or remembering the way you woke that particular morning before you fall asleep the next time. The most important feature of this exercise is that you find the way that is most natural for you. We only make active changes by owning what we are already doing. This ownership becomes the foundation for constructive change. After you have a fortnight's list of your waking-up methods and the pattern of the ensuing days, choose the ones you would like to continue and possibly develop. File them in a folder or shoe box and label them 'developing wake-ups'. Treat all others in the same manner and label them 'compost'. Next notice if there are any overlapping themes in the 'developing wake-ups' list and understand what those themes are telling you about yourself at the moment.

A month's worth of wake-up awareness begins a habit. Three months cultivates a cycle which becomes the beginning of a lifestyle. Note how natural observation has afforded you a more directed approach to your life. Note how your lifestyle is becoming more in tune with your instincts – and with what brings you more pleasure and a sense of purpose.

Morning Decisions and Daily Flow

The moment the alarm goes off we are faced with a myriad of decisions. Shall I get up or enjoy my nice warm bed a bit longer? What to wear? Breakfast . . . hum . . . shall I have a proper one or grab something on the way to work? Whether or not one realizes it these very simple, mundane decisions constitute the first stages of our participation in the flow of life. Every flow is initiated by a source of pressure – a force exerted from outside in or the reverse. The water starts running when we turn on the tap. Just as waves are drawn up by the moon's gravity, each of our decisions is initiated by a certain background of history or attitudes, as is each of our ways of interfacing with what we as a society have deemed 'normal'. Beyond the flow of our personal decisions are the events of the world which affect our lives in some way. The weather, economic conditions, transportation systems, and so on, are telescoped into our personal arenas the moment we choose to interface with the greater flow. What one fails to see, however, is that the way we make these basic personal decisions after we wake up actually sets the course for our days. Moreover, both attitudes towards our decisions as well as the way we interpret them as either opportunity or threat, over time accumulate as the chicken *and* the egg which reign over the quality of our lives. Again, who set the alarm anyway? Each of us has the power to make a masterpiece of our days, our lives – or to turn them to ashes.

By acknowledging some of the decisions made during your day you shed light on this integral part of life, and, as stated earlier, you effect a constructive change in this process. Which decision set off a chain of other decisions? Which one led to constructive and pleasurable results?

The two file headings for this section are:

1. decisions of draining consequence
2. decisions of meaningful consequence

The other half of this decision awareness is to notice how decisions based on 'I want' or 'I am interested in————' sharpened your sensitivity to the object of interest. This phenomenal relationship with our interest is clearly illustrated when one decides on a particular car and then, seemingly, out of nowhere, and all of a sudden, one begins to see that car everywhere. Similarly, when you decide you are attracted to a certain colour, then start seeing it in the most unusual places. I am suggesting here that whatever we focus on becomes the effect we receive. Consequently, what one continues to look for in life is what one gets. I know this inside out as a woman of mixed race. I used to use my race, age and sex as excuses for my inability to achieve desired results. As long as I maintained this victim posture, I continued to attract people to me who looked first at these externals and who wouldn't listen to anything I was saying as a result of this prejudice. When I woke up and looked at myself as someone who was here doing my work like everyone else, rather than a victim of society – (and yes, those prejudices do exist), but my sense of worth was such that they had nothing to do with me – I started attracting people into my life who responded to the calibre of my character. After some time, I would smile when some of these people from different backgrounds from mine had not only genuinely forgotten what race, sex, etc. I was, but what they were as well. All the social stereotypes disappeared as we got on with that to which we were each making valuable contributions.

The Way We Approach Life Affects the Outcome

The following exercise will give you a clear and immediate sense of how you programme yourself creates a certain climate of activity.

Exercise A
Without altering the normal position of your head, imagine that the roof of your mouth is closer to the ground that it is to the ceiling. (If you prefer, you can refer to your nose instead.) Walk around with this perspective for three minutes and notice:

(a) How are you breathing?
(b) What are you able to see, hear, smell and taste?
(c) What is your general feeling, your mood?
(d) How do you feel towards others in general and those in your immediate environment?
(e) What is the pace of your walk?
(f) If someone walked into the room and offered you something you needed, how receptive would you be to them?
(g) Does this way of walking remind you of any particular scene (on television, something you've seen at the theatre or in a certain area of life)?

Clear your palette by literally shaking your body as if shaking off water.

Exercise B

Now, again without altering the position of your head, walk around with the feeling that the roof of your mouth is closer to the ceiling than to the ground, for three minutes.

Go down the same list of questions and observe the differences in your response.

The general response to exercise A is shallow breathing, tunnel vision, a feeling of heaviness and depression, lack of awareness of others and the environment, lack of spontaneity and a slower pace. People often report the likeness of this disposition to that of a prison.

On the other hand, the response to exercise B is quite different. There are reports of deeper breathing, broader perspective, a feeling of lightness and joy, interest in others and the environment, more spontaneous expression, and a faster pace. The reason for the divergent responses is quite simple. Our thinking and our bodies are intimately linked. When we lower the ceiling of our perspective, i.e., the roof of mouth is closer to the ground, the body takes on the gravity of this intention.

Alternatively, when we raise the ceiling of our perspective the body responds in an uplifting way. The spine lengthens naturally which allows all the nerves travelling from the brain to the spine and all the muscles and organs to transmit our intentions more effectively. As the body becomes upright there is literally more room in the chest cavity for the lungs to operate efficiently, thus the sensation of deeper breathing and the quicker pace.

In both cases, nothing in your life was different. You still had the same responsibilities, the same problems, the same bills to pay, the same things you enjoy doing. Your attitude – your relationship with yourself is the only thing that changed – your body, your perceptions, your mood. With a little will power and concentration we can turn this into a way of life. When we can stay in touch with the impact of our attitudes we wake up to our potential. Our awareness becomes expanded. We become conscious. After all, there *is* no time like the present.

2

PLANNING AHEAD
The Tool: Expanded Awareness

**In this chapter we will realize tools for maximizing produc-
tivity – mentally, physically, materially, and spiritually. The
goal is peace of mind and a sense of well-being. This peace of
mind and well-being comes from within – from knowing and
living what is appropriate for you.**

The road to accepting total responsibility for one's life is not always a
bed of roses. And if it is, the roses certainly have thorns. However, the
rewards gained by living with one's eyes open, versus handing over
one's life to society, opiates, and others, are far greater.

> *A friend said to me: If you want the fruits from the tree, then you've
> got to go out onto the limb. So here I am . . . and I'll be back again.*
>
> MEG CHRISTIAN

If waking up is the needle on the path to reclaiming your power, then
expanded awareness is certainly the thread.

*Awareness combined with feeling is the substance by which we weave
the texture and quality of our lives.* After you have developed a working
relationship with your waking process, the next step is to familiar-
ize yourself with the mechanisms that organize your life – consciousness. Consciousness is the product of internalized awareness.
When we live what we know we become conscious. Consciousness
has been defined in many ways. As taking responsibility for our
lives is the premise of this book, I will define consciousness as the

embodiment of an idea. Here consciousness means living what one thinks and speaks. When perceived this way the notions of the subconscious or the neurological mechanism that draws our beliefs into manifestation, as well as the unconscious or seeds of awareness that are en route to becoming conscious, must be considered as part of an expanded awareness.

In this light we must take full responsibility for all parts of our lives. Under this definition we cannot be excused by saying such things as, 'Oh, I don't remember doing this or that. That isn't fitting with who I am. I must have been tipsy', nor are we allowed simply to relegate our sub- and unconscious selves to the skill of the psychiatrist. We must first recognize and own these parts of ourselves and they will emerge from the shadows of obscurity into our hands. Sometimes one requires help with different stages of this process. At these times, it is important that we seek skilled persons – ones who have reputations for not allowing us to hand over our power to them. Taking responsibility for the course of our lives is the most crucial step in claiming our power. Each of us taps the power of consciousness whenever we plan ahead for an activity, transition, or event in our lives. In this chapter we will realize/remember that it is possible to use consciousness as a dynamic force to shape the quality of our lives, on all levels. Once we are aware of what we are likely to encounter, we cease to be victims of circumstances. We can prepare to get the most out of the situation. Sometimes our thinking mind doesn't hold all the answers or the appropriate approach to obscure and troubling experiences. Sometimes we expedite insight by listening to more basic dimensions of ourselves such as our bodies and our dreams, and the language we use.

$$M = EC^2$$

M = manifested matter

E = emotion and energy directed towards a particular way of being (intention)

C^2 = concentrated love or inappropriate desires (lies) expressed over time

Thinking Becomes Believing, Believing Becomes Reality

After waking up we now go deeper into the adventure of taking charge of our lives through bringing into focus what it is that needs our attention, namely, energy. Increased energy in any direction, to any idea or object creates growth in that particular area.

In practical Taoist philosophy there is the idea that everything in existence was once three dots. Each of these dots represents a stage of development. Each of us has these three stages at our disposal. They are present in us before, during and after birth. When *acknowledged, cultivated* and *protected* consciousness expands in each area, as do the manifestations therein. This is the way the ancient Taoist philosophers explain the mystery behind reality. The first dot represents the idea of something and is described in simple terms as the *etheric* or *causal stage*. The belief here is that everything is caused by an idea. Idea material is light and invisible in its nature. If given enough attention the idea becomes denser as it enters the realm of the astral plane. At this point in time and space the idea becomes a feeling . . . a belief. The nature of the astral realm is sticky or attractive of all that is consistent with its desire. Our dreams are of the astral realm. When a belief reaches a certain pitch it becomes manifest. This constitutes the third and most dense phase of existence – physical formation or embodiment. So it follows with this blueprint that *what we think we become*.

THE THREE GATES OF ENLIGHTENMENT

These three stages, when in their most positive and mature states, correspond to three areas of life. They are referred to as gates or islands. **Wisdom** is the outcome of the clear ideas that lead us to the larger context. **Joy** is the expression of loving beliefs and harmonious relationships. **Wealth** is the product of conscientious embodiment. According to this philosophy there are three dimensions which are resources to these three states, and ones we

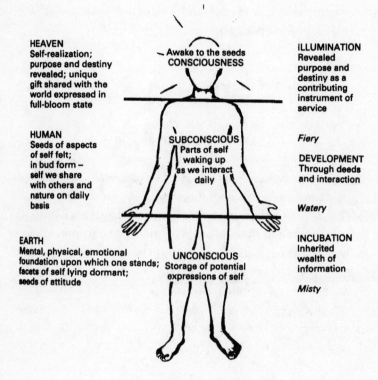

Figure 1 Power Consciousness

encounter daily. One can only be truly enlightened when *all three* are functioning fully. This position necessarily challenges the belief that spiritually must be exclusive of wealth and joy and the notion of 'the starving artist'. In the ancient Chinese martial art of Chi Kung the body is seen as a vehicle for these three dimensions of life. They provide a context for integration.

HEAVEN, HUMAN, EARTH – AWARENESS RESOURCES

The Heaven Dimension

The *heaven* dimension relates to the gate of wisdom and has to do with inspiration, insight and illumination. Our guides, teachers and angels speak to us through the heaven realm. Here is one lifted out of the mundane into the sublime. In astrology, the heaven realm is related to our star sign, our sense of purpose. The feeling is of excitement. The heaven realm has a quality of infinite possibilities. It is light, spacious and beautiful. When we relate the heaven realm to its source, the causal plane, we can see how the phrase 'heaven is in your mind' bears practical meaning. All that inspires us is of the heaven dimension.

Heaven in Our Bodies

The shape of the heaven realm, as interpreted energetically through our bodies, is that of a funnel with the widest part being above the head and the narrow pouring part in the base of the throat. It reverses direction and the pouring end seals off and becomes a point when one becomes realized, with the point of the triangle inside the head touching the crown. In one's vision quest this is the first step on the path. When one is operating consciously the heaven realm plants its seed into the human dimension.

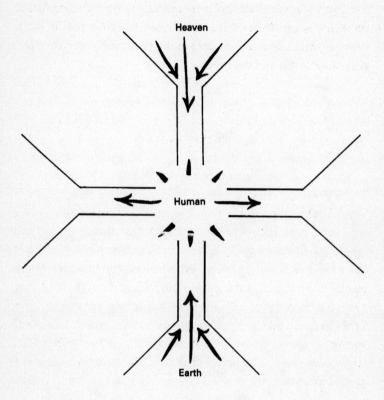

Figure 2 Consciousness Initiated Through the Three Realms

The Human Dimension

The *human* dimension relates to the gate of joy. This dimension has to do with the way we interact with the contents of our heaven realm and, consequently, rules our daily interactions with others and with the immediate societal rules. Astrologically speaking, the human realm related to the ascendant. The human realm is of the astral plane; the feeling quality is denser. In the human realm one gives and receives love; one expresses courage and compassion. Our daily interactions reflect our limitations and our strengths. Dealing with another person, bureaucracy, or rules, takes us into the denser material. Here is the testing ground of the idea. *Here is the opportunity for self-discovery – how we respond to others and to the world.*

The Human Dimension in Our Bodies

The human realm runs from the base of our throats down to our navels. The shape, as interpreted energetically through our bodies, is that of two funnels with the narrow, pouring parts facing each other in the centre of the chest. The human realm involves all the organs of the torso (heart, liver, lungs, stomach, spleen, gall bladder) and the heart and solar plexus chakras. As the heart is the centre of the human realm the flow is horizontal, emanating from the side and radiating from the heart. It relates to lateral thinking and action. Give and take come through these funnels of energy. The expression of love, courage and compassion comes from the centre of the heart. As is true of the heaven realm when one becomes realized, the funnels reverse and become sealed off at the ends. This means that the two triangles meet together to make a radiant diamond in the centre of the chest. The person becomes a living example of his or her ideas, the male and female of self are integrated into a harmonious union. Here then is a beacon in a new and universal way of being. The two large ends meet in the centre of the heart giving one the transformative power of love which is used for healing on a large scale. Those who are realized in the human realm know that everyone they encounter is a reflection of themselves. *In one's vision quest this is the second step on the path.* When one is operating consciously the human realm expresses the seeds of the heaven dimension whilst it receives the emotional/physical grounding of the earth dimension.

The Earth Dimension

The *earth* dimension relates to the gate of wealth and has to do with our connection with the earth and nature. It is through the earth dimension that we feel and manifest our sense of self in the world. Confidence is a quality we acquire when our relationship with the earth and nature is strong. In astrology, the earth realm relates to the moon or the nature of our emotional response to life. In the way of the shaman, it is through this realm that we meet our power animal. These are animals we may be attracted to or ones that recur in our dreams, sometimes in frightening ways. We are frightening by our power animal(s) because we are not consciously accepting their teachings. We are frightened by them when we haven't accepted their qualities within ourselves.

The earth dimension has to do with feeling connected and supported – a feeling of belonging. My bioenergetics counsellor, Alexandra Kennedy, once told me: 'When we feel deserted by everyone, even our mothers and best friends, we can lie on the earth and she will support us.' It is in the earth dimension that we have the 'leg to stand on' in an argument or when we are selling our ideas and skills. The earth dimension is about having what it takes and the push from below and inside to make it happen. In short, it is about reality. This is why it is the densest realm in the stages of reality and is the envoy of manifestation. This is the third step in the vision quest. Here is the realization of the idea. The next step is to harvest and then to improve and refine these qualities in areas of self. Here is the opportunity for self-actualization – of coming to terms with and living the reality of our unique purpose. Reflection on what we have on a daily basis versus what we don't have is the quickest route to the earth realm.

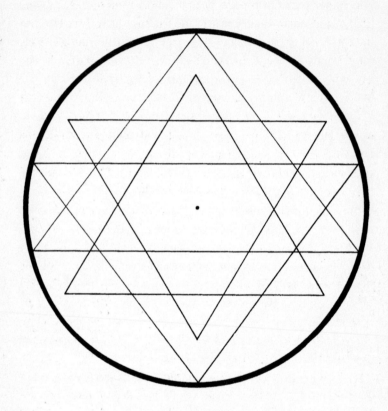

Figure 3 Heaven, Human, Earth Realized

The Earth Dimension in Our Bodies

The human realm represents the foundation of our bodies and runs from our navels through our legs and feet to at least three feet into the earth. For those without legs or feet the earth realm still exists from the navel through the lower body, three feet into the earth. The shape of the earth realm as interpreted energetically through our bodies is that of a funnel with the widest part three feet into the earth with the narrow pouring parts facing our navels. The human realm involves the energy channels of the legs and feet, the sexual organs and the intestines. It overlaps with the human region in that it specifically includes the stomach and spleen. (In Chinese medicine these are considered earth organs). The other purpose of the earth realm is to nourish and to ground volatile thoughts, energies and emotions. The kidneys are other organs shared by the earth and human realms as they provide nourishment and grounding through regulating and purifying the major composition of our bodies – the water. The earth realm includes the root and spleen chakras. Creativity, sexual pleasure, and giving birth are functions of the earth realm as well. Unlike the heaven and human realms, when one becomes realized the funnel maintains its original position. However, the base does become larger according to the person's evolution and sphere of influence. In addition, another triangle is superimposed on the wealth triangle but in reverse position. Together they form a six-pointed star which is the emblem of enlightenment. Idea has become reality. As above, so below. The power of this organization can be meditated upon with the Sri Yantra which is a visual representation of the holy OM vibration. The Sri Yantra is a series of overlapping triangles, some pointing upwards some pointing down. It describes the embodiment of all three planes or reality. At this point, one crosses the threshold of spiritual-material mastery. The greatest product of the earth realm is self-realization as the earth realm is the product of the previous two. Again, the person becomes a living example of his or her ideas and can effectively instruct others in these ways. One's thoughts, words and actions are magnetic. Some may think of this as magic. This is another way of giving away our potential to manifest fulfilling lives. There is indeed a method and science underlying 'reality'. This type of mass belief or consensus reality contributes to whatever we have collectively agreed to be reality.

The whole is as great as the sum of the *quality* of its parts.

Women and Earth Power

In my work with women I have found the mature expression of the earth dimension (self-realization) to be the most challenging. We are encouraged to use our earth power to bear children. For some of us this *is* part of self-realization. For others of us it is a convenient distraction which we become drawn into right on the brink of giving birth to ourselves. Because of pain, societal conditioning and shame associated with the ovarian and womb power centres, we have literally lost power in this area. I watch women who are about to manifest their power in the world become pregnant. It is too scary for many of us to feel this power, to not fit in. We feel vulnerable and unsupported in this way. Becoming pregnant is the easy way to ground the initial volatile energies involved in giving birth to one's greater potential. It takes courage and deep strength to overcome this compulsion. The consensus reality hasn't quite awakened to the benefit to all that this support will provide. Women and men are equally responsible for this denial. In his brilliant work of scholarship, *Return of the Goddess*, Edward C. Whitmont describes the importance in our reclaiming the power of the earth centre. He explains the association of the earth realm with hell. It is our complete responsibility to transmute this belief and bring more of heaven into the earth realm. This is one of our greatest powers. When it becomes utilized by consensus we all evolve. Work in the earth realm, with our legs, feet and navel centres is a start in the development of this strength.

Review:

Facets of the Heaven Realm

- inspiration
- hope
- intuition
- vision beyond appearances
- guides, teachers, angels/the higher self
- understanding of the balance of yin and yang
- protective guidance
- a sense of authority
- one's religion/morals/ethics
- aesthetics
- flashes of creative insight

Facets of the Human Realm

- affairs of the heart – the ability to give and receive love, to express courage and compassion
- artistic painting and music composition
- general give and take balance
- expression of the balance of yin and yang
- maintenance activities as we interface with societal rules
- general correspondence and communication

Facets of the Earth Realm

- confidence
- health
- money
- wealth
- survival instinct
- creativity
- passion

- a sense of purpose
- 'having a leg to stand on'
- sense of background – heritage/ancestry
- one's relationship with animals (in shaman's terms, one's power animals)
- our connection with nature and the collective unconscious
- our dreams
- mobility
- power to grow
- practical skills
- instinct
- writing

These three realms are tools by which we may organize, study and refine their respective areas of our lives. You might notice which areas are stronger, which are weaker and how they came to be that way. You might also pay attention to the possibility that one or some have been stronger at different times in your life, and review which events or turning points precipitated their strength. Awareness and investigation of this nature produce consciousness and provide us with useful information to plan ahead.

To summarize, these three levels and their respective origins (the three dots) can be used as an outline for expanded awareness and self-development. Feel into these three areas in your body. Where are you strong? Where are you weak? What can you do to galvanize your strengths. What can you do to strengthen the weaker parts, *mentally, emotionally, physically, nutritionally, environmentally?* Take stock of what you have and build from there. Which ideas, people, places, foods, and music nourish each realm for you?

CULTIVATING CONSCIOUSNESS

The ways to cultivating consciousness are many. Here are some basic areas which are immediately accessible and provide maps to consciousness development. First, I would like to address one of the prevailing attitudes which I feel inhibits consciousness.

Words on the Mind over Body Idea and Practice

We are often encouraged to maintain a stiff upper lip as a sign of strength at all times. This is fine as long as the stiffness doesn't repress signals from our bodies and emotions that something is threatening our well-being. It is fine as long as these emotions and physical responses have an outlet of expression.

One problem I see with any spiritual idealism that suggests that the body is bad and of lower intelligence – lower importance than the mind – is that it cuts us off from the intelligence of the body. *If we were meant to be purely spiritual we would not live in bodies.*

Our minds are powerful. We have already seen how strongly the attitude of mind works with the body in the roof of the mouth exercise. The difference in the use of this exercise, as a way of changing how we frame our experience at each moment, is that the mind and body were working in harmony. The mind wasn't dominating the body, it was cooperating with it.

The neurophysiologist John Eccles has been quoted as saying: 'We pride ourselves as being superior to animals with our large cerebrums – our reasoning power. This is why we are so capable or technological feats such as going to the moon, flying aeroplanes, and creating computers. Yet with our great cerebrums we still have murder and war. Our reasoning power is out of balance with our motives.'

Joseph Campbell in his *The Power of Myth* (Doubleday, 1988) says that 'the thinking mind should never be put in control'. He goes on to say that 'when we allow the mind to be in control at the expense of the body and emotions schizophrenia develops'.

Unless one is an athlete there is a split between our physical and mental drives. And we have suppressed the intelligence of the body to the extent that we have disease and psychological problems. This is not to suggest, however, that everyone would be better off as an athlete. the suggestion is that we listen to our bodies – to communicate with them in ways which increase our joy of life; that we increase the sensitivity of our bodies so that they let us know when we are out of alignment with our vital purposes. This, of course, is a very personal decision.

Consciousness Expressed through Our Bodies

Pain, injuries and disease in particular parts of our bodies are expressions of the intelligence of the body and can be used as keys into the flow of our lives. This happens in several ways:

1. We are not paying attention to our basic needs at the time so the body breaks down to reprimand us into changing.

2. We are growing or changing levels at a more rapid rate than those around us so there is added stress due to lack of support. The reverse of this is also a possibility, that, is, we have moved to a more stimulating environment or are receiving a great deal of love after suffering hurt so the body is growing rapidly to accommodate the expansion in consciousness.

3. We are predisposed to certain ailments through our DNA or through strong identification with a parent (a form of ancestral physical imprinting).

PAIN AND PLEASURE AS THE MASTER TEACHERS OF CONSCIOUSNESS EXPRESSED THROUGH THE BODY

When we fail to pay attention to our natural course our bodies let us know.

As mentioned earlier, the body has its own intelligence. The major way it talks to us is through heightened sensation in particular areas. One experience of this is that we feel more comfort or pleasure; in the other, there is discomfort or pain. How one grows from either of these is reflective of individual self-esteem. Those who tend to grow from pain display lower self-esteem while others who grow from pleasurable experiences display a higher regard for themselves. The interpretative list below will give you clues as to what your consciousness is telling you through your body. Pain, injury or disease in any of these areas implies a need to let go of the old to make room for the new. Increased pleasurable sensations indicate an evolutionary awakening – one for which you have been preparing or with which you have been cooperating:

head – change of perspective; rigid thought forms, held anger;

lower back of head – vision of the future;

top/crown of head – heavy morals, false authorities, listening to one's source;

back of neck – you are letting someone pull you back or are giving your power away by letting them speak for you;

throat – need to express something important to you;

shoulders – carrying too much responsibility or someone else's; need to carry more responsibility;

hands – need to make contact with others, with the world;

wrists and shoulder joint – these are the bridges between the heart and the world. Pain or loosening in both describes a conflict of flow between the contents of the heart and our ability and inclination to share with others;

chest/lungs – grief, feeling crowded, lack of freedom, wish to support oneself in the world;

centre/heart – longing for ideal love; unconditional love, courage to be self; compassion and forgiveness;

spine – truth, alignment with true identity;

lower spine – connection with one's roots, blocked deep-seated sexual power; heritage;

stomach – grounding; home; nurturing;

kidneys – will power, relationships that drain one's vitality, fear of failure;

intestines – general fear, guilt, living from one's instincts, one's dreams, lack of fulfilment;

pelvis and hips – creativity, pleasure, power base, expansion, travel, enthusiasm (*left side*: expansion in home and personal identity; *right side*: expansion in the world, covering more territory, selling oneself);

buttocks – power to propel oneself forward;

thighs/long upper leg muscles – stamina, concentration;

knees – changing levels (*left*: at home, in self; *right*: in work); also dealing with the internalized messages from our parents (*left*: the mother; *right*: the father and authority figures);

calves – clarification of universal truths including one's personal visions;

feet – connection with the earth, one's roots/motives, grounding, and one's connection with all humanity.

Planning Cultivates Consciousness

We have all exercised the use of consciousness in any act of planning. When planning for something we desire we look at the steps from different angles. We examine our strengths and weaknesses. We prepare for obstacles. We accentuate activity that will produce the greatest results.

There are clear examples of this illusive dimension of ourselves, or consciousness, all around us. The business-minded person plots every interaction around the greatest financial returns. A landscape artist organizes the garden around the seasons for the greatest year-round visual pleasure. Symbiotic plants are placed to enhance each other's growth and well-being. (Whilst working in the vineyards in California, I learned specific seasonal rituals to promote the long-term productivity of the vines: pruning in late winter strengthens the longevity of the vine's stem structure and root strength; suckering in the early summer or removing the appropriate green shoots encourages the plant's to produce succulent mature grapes.) The athlete trains to warm up the muscle groups needed for the particular game to increase performance. Planned parenthood is all about ensuring the balanced distribution of care between parents and child. Each of these examples speaks of consciousness. Each of these is an item in the index file of consciousness – which brings me to the next point. Consciousness tends to be catalysed around either (1) an area of interest such as athletics and gardening or (2) an event such as having a child or obtaining life insurance. All the examples mentioned above are positive and life-affirming. Consciousness, as we all well know, can be used for destructive means such as conspiracies and genocide. Again, in both cases, positive and negative, it is organized around an area of interest or an event (history and politics).

ANOTHER AMONG THEM

Jane, a Keeper of the Arts and Music

Her discriminating mind gave her the ability to use her resources and her power to keep the candles of inspiration burning for all of us – art, music, and self-help preventive health care.

Consciousness as Choice

The more we realize that everything is temporary, the more fluid our operation is with ourselves (pain is an example, so are emotions) and the world. It is by living merely through our personalities that we adhere to a certain way of being. Stability and integrity are useful as long as, through their use in our lives, we continue to prosper and feel well. It is possible to feel stable whilst being in the pits of despair, as long as one is aware of using the despair as a means of growing. It is also possible to feel this well-being whilst in a moment of orgasmic ecstasy, and again, as long as it is appreciated as a temporary state or food for the development of one's purpose. Often, in the reflective aspects of my classes, students report visions or beautiful scenery or hear sounds which they refer to as celestial. I always congratulate them for giving themselves permission to 'open up' while at the same time encouraging them to enjoy these displays as by-products of the deeper feeling of peace, rather than to be side-tracked by these experiences. We are capable of choosing the lens through which we view our experiences, both the painful and the joyous.

Consciousness as the Way We Respond to Opportunity

When you're movin' in the positive, your destination is the brightest star.

STEVIE WONDER

In discussing such an illusive topic one cannot ignore the fact that there are people living in horrific conditions. All who read this book are privileged to have the opportunity for self-improvement. Just as in self-defence classes, I am not suggesting that one who has been attacked asked for it, nor am I suggesting that people who are starving or tortured are asking for it. And yet, although the suggestions here are for those of us who are not living under constant life-threatening conditions, in the remote chance that those who are have an opportunity to entertain these tools, I do feel they would be of benefit.

We are surrounded by opportunities. As was demonstrated in the roof of the mouth exercise in Chapter 1, the attitudes held within our bodies can determine the quality of our immediate experience.

Everything that happens in our lives is part of a larger plan. When we expect this to be true we increase our peace of mind and sense of security. Constant change then becomes accepted as part and parcel of the flow of life. When we split our experiences into 'good' or 'bad' we break the thread of flow and increase our suffering. Suffering is a product of an inability to grow or move on. Looking at our experiences merely through our personalities inhibits growth and confines us to the treadmill of repetitive patterns which keep us limited.

Courage Is Required for Conscious Living

It takes courage to wake up and live in consciousness. For many of us the attachment of belonging to a particular group or person can keep us from flowing gracefully to our destinies, even when that group or person no longer feels healthy for us on a gut level. We fear that if we listen to our innermost impulses to respond to opportunities we will be lonely and unloved. I know this feeling well. In an attempt to retrieve the parts of self which my personality felt were being put down, I dedicated fifteen years of my life to the black and women's movements. I am happy to have done so as they were both enriching experiences. Both reminded me of something I knew as a child, that I am fine just the way I am – skin colour, heritage and gender. These bits of self seemed lost as I interfaced with the values of society. I am even happier that I had the courage to recognize when both these movements had provided me with the strength to go back into society to carry on with my destiny, rather than becoming limited and insulated from the world in these wombs of acceptance and isolation. To stay in each movement I would have had to fuel my anger continually. Wounds healed, then other parts of me cried out to be expressed. I am a person who must live in the world. However, each time I stood on the threshold of change I wondered if there would be anyone where I was going – if I would end up being alone and without support, now that I felt the need to depart from these supportive subgroups of society. Each time I leap I find a whole host of people of similar values. New friends in greater abundance and greater integrity wonder where I have been. This tells me I am now ready and willing to live these parts of myself – those I have attracted in others.

The most difficult part of taking growth-oriented steps is making the leap, confronting the abyss. There are times when we have to weigh opportunities to grow with our involvements with others. Our loved ones become crucial barometers against which we measure the rewards of our own growth. I have found that the more we respond to opportunities that genuinely feel right for us, we discover who our loved ones truly are. Over time people who love us overcome personal insecurities and love and respect us even more for having the courage to be who we really are. Alternatively, we discover that our destinies may be different after all. Waking up and living consciously is not always an easy task, especially in taking the first step. It can mean that we have to question and change the people, places the things we have been holding on to to maintain the security to which the limited self has grown so attached. It can mean starting all over again just when we thought we were getting into our stride. Self-esteem plays a major role in augmenting or minimizing the amount of upheaval associated with living consciously. Self-esteem combines one's thinking power with one's instincts and appreciation of uniqueness. The more conscious we become the more our self-esteem increases and we attract loved ones who are in harmony with our destinies, rather than those who scorn us for living our truth. After several attempts one comes through to the other side and trust in the inner urge to move on grows stronger. The frozen image of self melts and a new more inclusive self is born. Kahlil Gibran describes this growth process with profound eloquence in the following passage from his *Garden of the Prophet*:

Then Sarkis, he who was the half-doubter, spoke and said: 'But Spring shall come, and all the snows of our dreams and our thoughts shall melt and be no more.'

'So shall the snow of your heart melt when your Spring is come, and thus shall your secret run in streams to seek the river of life in

the valley. And the river shall enfold your secret and carry it to the great sea.'

'All things shall melt and turn into stars when Spring comes. Even the stars, the vast snow-flakes that fall slowly upon the larger fields, shall melt into singing streams. When the Spring's face shall rise above the wider horizon, then what frozen symmetry would not turn into liquid melody?'

The more we respond to opportunities to grow, the more conscious we become. The more our lives begin to align with our gut feelings and intuitions and visions, and the more we remember why we are here. As our ability to respond to opportunities develops, we augment our awakening process and stand taller in a sense of purpose.

Consciousness through Our Feet and Hands

We can increase the basic sensation of consciousness simply by being more aware of our feet. Actually feeling sensations of life in our feet such as warmth, tingling and pulsing allow us to be more connected to the ground, to ourselves and to each other. Many have found this modest observation to be evolutionary in their lives. Reports such as a genuine connection with all humanity, increased compassion, and clues to solving personal problems coming through a smile from a stranger walking along the road, or an advert in tube stations, are common responses to insights that come from more attention to the feet. One person says he uses his feet to tell him if he is entering into a solid business deal. Whenever he has had cold feet the deal has fallen through. Warm and tingling feet during the transactions have always proved success. The more we relate to our feet, and after all they do literally support us, the more they will serve us. They become radar systems. So is it true with our hands also.

Consciousness Expressed through Our Dreams

Our dream worlds are the windows into our subconscious self as they are a reflection of our beliefs. Again, our beliefs are the strongest of our manifesting powers and are the bridge between the causal and manifestation planes of reality. Our *psyches* are the messages or these three stages of reality. One might describe the psyche metaphorically as the RNA to our reality DNA. The three planes hold the potential and the psyche is how we carry it out. Evolution of our potential is the intent of the psyche. It overrides the limitations of our personalities and limited egos. It keeps us aligned with the greater reality of our destinations.

At a higher level of consciousness our dreams and waking 'reality' are indistinct. This points to the importance of their value in the development of our expanded awareness. The three dimensions of heaven, human and earth create the outline for dream study.

Earth Realm Dreams
Generally speaking, any dreams where the direction is downward – going downstairs, falling, planes coming down, downward shooting stars, going into basements, under water, etc. – are of the earth realm. Dreams of this nature, especially if they are recurring, speak of the need to become more grounded in the qualities described earlier of the earth dimension. The psyche is telling us to go under for a while, to become emotionally grounded in the ideas we are entertaining.

Human Realm Dreams
Dreams of mundane activities such as going to the market, paying one's bills, the worksite, and relationships, are of the human realm. The psyche is telling us of the need to put more focus into these aspects of our life.

Heaven Realm Dreams
When we have those wonderful flying dreams, ones of rising up,

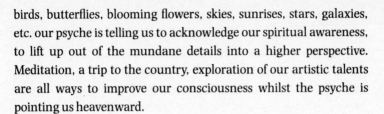

birds, butterflies, blooming flowers, skies, sunrises, stars, galaxies, etc. our psyche is telling us to acknowledge our spiritual awareness, to lift up out of the mundane details into a higher perspective. Meditation, a trip to the country, exploration of our artistic talents are all ways to improve our consciousness whilst the psyche is pointing us heavenward.

Recurring Dreams of Home and Familiar People
Our dream world is the special time for us to fly freely into the well-spring of our greater selves. Dreams of rooms in our houses, and of the people who live with us, indicate we are feeling stuck or frustrated, or that we are repressing ourselves in some way.

Consciousness and Karma:
What We Reap Is What We Have Sown

I strongly believe that if, even for a moment, each of us realized that for every underlying desire we have there is a consequence – one that comes back to be recycled through us – we might be more willing to structure our desires strategically for the greatest beneficial returns. We would also be more careful of the nature of our desires. In this chapter we will explore our deepest impulses and realize tools for maximizing our returns – mentally, physically, materially, and spiritually.

Within each of us there is a rich well-spring of our potential, which resides in our DNA, our gut feelings, and in our visions of the future. The essential return is peace of mind and a sense of well-being, qualities which arise when we uncover and discriminate the 'wheat from the chaff' in these areas. A lifestyle imbued with one's greatness develops when we trust and act on these vital parts of self.

Consciousness as the Atmosphere We Create

We each have an effect on our immediate environment as it does on us. Have you ever noticed how some people can light up a gloomy crowd when they enter the room, while others bring in the clouds? It is easy to relinquish responsibility for our potential by thinking that star-type people are naturally gifted in this respect, as are those with a depressing nature. Each of us has the ability to create both these atmospheres; this was demonstrated in Chapter 1 in the roof of the mouth exercise. As Rev. Rosalyn Bruyere says, 'Consciousness is contagious in the field.' When we are constantly surrounded by depressing environments, without light and fresh air, in which there is prevalence of hostility or cigarette smoke, we gradually lose energy and become depressed. The more conscious a person is the sooner the effects are noticed. The more fresh air, light, greenery and conviviality, the more harmonious we are with ourselves and with each other. When we are physically active and alive in our bodies, as well as our minds, we create a fresher atmosphere around us. The more conscious a person is, the more he or she wishes to be in this quality of setting, and the greater the self-esteem as a result. Consciousness is also expressed by the thoughts and conversations we have. When we feed our minds with beauty and life-supporting information, we exude the same atmosphere – the same applies to angry, judgemental and gossipy thoughts. By improving our internal energies on both a mental and physical level, we affect our emotional and spiritual balance and exude an aura that is pleasant and healing in its effect.

The Enemies of Consciousness

There are certain way of thinking and behaving that distract us from the greater picture:

1. Low self-esteem.

2. The inability to respond to opportunity (rather than catering to the lowest common denominator). As women we are encouraged to cater to everyone who is needy rather than towards strength and excellence. Consequently, a woman who

has impulses to succeed in areas other than service to the needy, tends to inhibit herself with fears/judgements of being selfish and arrogant. Hence the saying: men kill their weak while women kill their strong.

3. Envy and jealousy of others distracts us from our purpose.

4. Internalizing information that decreases our sense of well-being: mentally, physically, emotionally, instinctively, intuitively.

5. Resistance to necessary changes and thus the need to control.

6. Denial of our heritage and of our potential.

Evolving Consciousness

There are two major ways I have found to quicken our expanded awareness:

1. When you detect a pattern of behaviour that prolongs suffering, break it. Whether it be a relationship pattern, a route to anything, do it in a different way. Get out of bed a different way. Listen a bit longer than usual in arguments.

2. Learn from those who practise what they preach first and foremost, and listen to all others to expand your sense of what is possible.

PART TWO

≈

3

CONSOLIDATING RESOURCES
the Tool: Power

Any great spirit which is truly evolving will, at times, subject itself to the most oppressive of forces for deeper strengthening and integration. The integration happens when the person involved recognizes the talents that have been gleaned from these dark hours and then emerges from the cocoon with mastery on her wings.

Every time we overcome an obstacle or meet a challenge we gain power.

Knowledge – choice – vehicles – tools – petrol – money – music – humour – knowing the right people – spirit – kindness – love – beauty – wisdom – inspiration – wealth – meditation – truth

These are all forms of power.

Whether it is getting the job you want, the partner, the love, the money, the life dream, developing that suspected talent, etc., one needs the right fuel to make it happen.

With your waking process now well in tow, the next step is to consolidate your resources – to recognize your power. This means recognizing what it takes to get the job done and utilizing the appropriate means. In Chapter 3 we explore your relationship with power.

WARNING

If you have any notions of using this information to hurt or manipulate others you may be in for a most unpleasant

surprise! Here power is about self-responsibility, utilizing it to maximize your potential, the greater you.

Beware the Power Frauds or people who use power to mask inadequacy, fear, lack of confidence. They are:

- **Exclusivity-mongers – privileged people who use language, social privilege, age, or gender to put other people down.**

- **People who become aggressive and verbally abusive to purport importance. They are usually trying to prevent you from discovering their mistakes or lack of solid information.**

- **People who deny pain and vulnerability.**

- **People who think other people, animals and resources are stupid simply because they are open, kind and loving. These people are projecting their own insecurities about being open.**

- **People who need to gossip and put others down without reason to feel better about themselves. These people's lives are barren.**

- **People who steal and exploit others' resources without paying respect to those resources because they do not recognize their own.**

- **People who are immediately prejudiced by colour, class, gender.**

- **People who boast and intimidate with intellect and ideas, with nothing to demonstrate.**

- **People who believe the human race to be superior to animals and the earth. They are in for a big surprise!**

- **Men who destroy the more sensitive and vulnerable of their gender.**

- **Women who destroy the more ambitious and strong leaders of their gender.**

- **Adults who think children should be seen, not heard.**

- **Adults who deny children their childhood, and, consequently, the child in themselves.**

The basic unit of power is energy. Energy is the most direct product of consciousness or the plan. Perhaps it will help to see the relationship between power and consciousness through the following metaphor: if waking up is the needle and consciousness is the thread, then power is the cloth. In this chapter we will look at the many faces of power, some of the myths about power and conclude with developing appropriate strategies for achieving the results your consciousness prescribes.

We all know that if we wish to get from point A to point B that some form of mobilization is necessary. It is also no surprise that there are a number of possible ways to get there. Mobilization requires energy. When we use energy to achieve impact we are using power. Both the impact and effect we have depends on the intention and the means we use.

Energy has many expressions. There are certain progressions of energy that either minimize or maximize its life-span. We will begin by looking at some of the major myths about power that may have distracted some of us from being in charge of our lives.

MYTHS ABOUT POWER

MYTH One must be selfish and arrogant to think about power.

FACT There are many types of power. We accrue power every time we overcome an obstacle or meet a challenge. I am reminded of the lines of a song by singer/songwriter Holly Near:

Linger on the details, the parts that reflect the change. There lies revolution. Our everyday lives, the changes inside become our political songs.

And yes, like anything it is possible to use power at the expense of others. The power I am addressing is about self-responsibility. The use of energy is for personal fulfilment which, when consciously executed, cannot be at the expense of others. The most lasting power is directed towards the benefit of all.

MYTH Power corrupts and absolute power corrupts absolutely.
FACT This myth points to the power which is synonymous with politics. It is an expression of power that may be used for corrupt ends. Power, like electricity, gunpowder, and money, has no mind of its own. Its expression lies strictly within the intentions of the user.

MYTH You will be knocked down by people or some form of divine intelligence if you exercise your power.
FACT This does happen to people who have the courage to speak the truth when it is threatening to those in positions of power. It also happens to each of us when we deny our power. The same also occurs when we change; the people who are attached to us can find the change threatening, though usually as a result of the repression of their growth. When we fear power for these reasons we become victims caught in the shackles of denial. One must choose which is more suitable. An awareness of the above can be empowering. Having choice is empowering. One can choose a timing and approach to stand up for one's beliefs which will minimize the threat.

MYTH Becoming in charge of one's life or empowered is arrogance and negates religion.
FACT This depends on your religion.

First, let's look at the major expressions of energy. We will begin with the most fundamental and purest structure of energy, the basic forces of power which are receiving and giving or yin and yang. These two recently popularized ancient Chinese concepts come by many names.

Yin		Yang
receptive		active
earth		heaven
watery		fiery
reflective		radiant
below	—	above
body		mind
dense	M	light
inspired thought		deep feeling
welcoming	A	sending
drawing in		pushing out
left	G	right
listening		directing
embracing	N	thrusting
leading		following
nurturing	E	providing
intuition		instinct
channel	T	force
detail		perspective
soothing	I	invigorating
cooling		heating
acquiescent/satisfied	C	ambitious
quietly calculating		direct inquisition
insinuation	—	directly stating
negative		positive
contracting		expanding
calm		excited
charisma		radiance
soft		hard

When both yin and yang qualities are in balance one becomes magnetic. All that one truly has need of comes. The state of joy becomes the power behind directional strength.

One of the most widespread misconceptions is that yin is female and yang is male. This is an unfortunate assumption as it inhibits total expression of both sides of energy in both sexes. The notion of yin and yang originated in the Eastern philosophy of Taoism. The essence of Taoism explains that one cannot be truly healthy, realized or whole until both these forces are balanced and in harmony. In martial arts it is the unexpressed force that has the greatest potential.

During the course of our lives each of us may have felt one of them as dominant in different times, body areas, and geographical locations. This is normal and healthy. When both forces are allowed to express themselves in the areas and spheres of influence that bring fulfilment, we have the power to flow with the changes in life. When we stifle one or the other in order to fit in with others' values, we become unbalanced which can lead to disease and dysfunction.

Yin and yang are essentially genderless. They describe the dynamic of the three stages of reality and integration. They originate from heaven or the 'giving' principle and earth or the 'receiving' principle. Another misconception is that (1) the yin force is passive and (2) that negative is interpreted as bad. The yin force actively expresses its nature just as the yang force comfortably expresses its own. The terms 'negative' and 'positive' refer to the drawing in and emitting aspect of yin and yang respectively. 'Good' and 'bad' are products of social values. Both expressions, yin and yang, are integrated in the navel or centre and are transmitted through the heart which is neutral.

Thus it follows that everything which comes from heaven or above is *provisional and temporary*, while everything which comes from earth is nurtured and *develops over time*. For instance, sunshine, rain, thunder and lightning come from heaven and are temporary in their expression. Each has its role in providing for an ecological need. Heaven is closest to idea. Heavenly exponents vibrate at a rapid rate. One's whole life orientation and way of thinking must be geared towards evolution if one is to live in the heavenly realm. Otherwise, one is subject to the pull of the earth's gravity which is more concerned with the material world and is of a denser nature and slower vibration.

Earth, on the other hand, receives each of these heavenly expressions, absorbs their influence and translates them into its entire nature then reflects back this absorption through fruitfulness. Trees, flowers, animals, fish, reptiles, insects, humans are all creatures of the earth and retain these properties. When provided for and nurtured we grow and prosper over time.

SEXUALITY AND POWER

One cannot discuss power without paying some respect to sexuality. The idea and life practice that women and girls are yin and men and boys are yang may have originated in the most primitive evidence of our difference in gender – the genitals and the basic characteristics they display when sexual energy is heightened, excited and in the presence of each other. The penis stiffens and the vulva and vagina soften, become moist and open. Also the process of impregnating wherein it appears that the sperm sends and the ovum receives. Prenatal studies are now showing that the ovum has a much more active role in choosing the sperm than was previously thought. This, however, is strictly a heterosexual dynamic, one which is taught and socially reinforced with great ardour. Who is to know how we would respond to this creative force in us if we were left to our own *natural* expression. In any case, sexuality is the most primitive use of power. Though it may be a means to creativity, it is not the end. I refer to this categorical definition as 'primitive' not as a judgement of sexuality, but because of the limited lens through which energy is viewed and the ensuing social ramifications. What is valued in this definition is procreation under the guise of promoting the family tree but really for the purpose of propagating the supply for the machinery of the social/economic system.

POWER POTENTIAL

Our potential for using power is ever expanding. Look at the use of plutonium, for example; from just a tiny drop it has tremendous potential to serve or destroy. Each of us has this plutonian power inside us. Every time our little ideas manifest, we are using plutonian power. Every time we realize the strength and insight we have gained from overcoming obstacles, we are employing plutonian power. Every time a child is born, we are using plutonian power. In our gardens, whenever we plant seeds and cultivate them into flowers, we are using plutonian power. How, then, can the male artist value his process of giving birth or the office manager, whether male or female, find fulfilment in taking care of the company family with such a categorical definition? The *invisible* motives behind energetic expression are equally viable and potent as demonstrated when a mother organizes a family outing, when she prepares and cooks a meal, and when the business man quietly calculates the timing to initiate a new deal. Such is true of the father who cuddles and nurtures the children and of the woman who is the 'brains' behind a successful enterprise. Each of these expressions of yang and yin achieves results. They have impact. The expressions are interchangeable relative to gender, depending on the individual's chemistry. Deeper than diet, stress and environmental pollutants, and perhaps closer to the root of the rising incidences of impotence in men and breast cancer in women is this rigidity in roles, the 'proper' energetic expression. Women who deny ambitious impulses and are guilt-ridden with the accepted role of being the nurturing one, or essentially breast feeding all the time, are in energetic/emotional conflict which must find a resolution through some means. Likewise men who are guilt-ridden for needing to be more receptive in the area of physical expression – the need to be 'big and butch' all the time – are masking the yin side and are, therefore, more susceptible to the yin expression when it is least desired, i.e. listlessness and impotence. Both acts of nurturing and providing are only powerful and enduring when the other side is equally present and expressed in some area of life.

When the two forces are accepted and expressed one is literally 'in charge' because yin and yang, like positive and negative aspects of electrical currents, create a charge. Two dominant energies of the same nature eventually drain each other whether it be between a woman and man, two women or two men. Energies that are complementary spark each other. It is up to each of us to recognize where our yin and yang are optimally expressed and to recognize and act upon them when and if they change. This is a vital step in reclaiming one's power.

The Yin-Yang Channels in Our Bodies

The yang or *governor* channel runs up from the base of the spine through the crown and down to the inner eye or the point between the eyebrows. Its function is to energize and increase the energy flow to the brain and nervous system to enhance alertness. The yin or *functional* channel runs downward from the throat to the perineum. Its function is to relax the respiratory and digestive organs for greater efficiency. Both channels are connected through the perineum and the tongue which rests in one of three positions on the roof of the mouth. The starting and ending point of the flow is the lower tan-tien or navel centre. When energy is balanced in both channels energy is increased and one is imbued with a feeling of well-being and a pleasant state of mind.

When genuinely felt, our smiles are an expression of these two channels in balance. Heaven or the upward pull is contained in the cup-like shape of the mouth representing earth infused with heaven. Babies of all cultural backgrounds naturally respond to this ambience of harmony.

When we are in the womb both forces are in a state of balance via

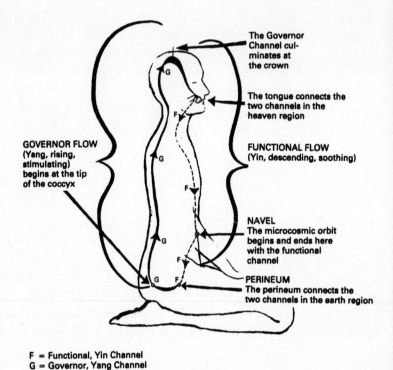

F = Functional, Yin Channel
G = Governor, Yang Channel

Figure 4 The Balancing Path of the Microcosmic Orbit

the umbilical cord, but after our arrival in the world the balance is usually tipped one way or the other. When we are born we learn very quickly to adapt to the conditions of our immediate environment, adopting behaviour that enables us to secure the love, food and shelter we need to survive. This conditioning makes a deep impression on the way we relate to ourselves and our power. It can also have an impact on our sense of destiny. We learn to follow the herd quietly or we wake up to our unique purposes. Once we are out of the nest we either step on to the path of self-discovery, realizing the essence of self that lies under the conditioning and in so doing align with our destinies, or we succumb further to that conditioning and accept it as our destinies.

The Microcosmic Orbit

The Taoist healing exercise, the 'microcosmic orbit', is both an outline and a training practice for cultivating the balance of yin and yang from within. The theory is that each of us is a microcosm of the universe or united idea. When we are balanced inside our lives take on this equilibrium. We become magnetic and attract everything we need, repulsing what is of no use to us. In this way, the balance of yin and yang strengthens our immune systems making us more resistant to disease – physical, mental and emotional. The microcosmic orbit is the major chi circuit which runs through the body, with concentrated energy centres like little towns along its route.

Take an Inventory and Chart your Energy

Exercise
This can be fun and a rewarding exercise in revealing ways in which you express your yin/yang forces.

Preparation and Necessary Supplies
You will need about two hours of quiet uninterrupted time. You may do this exercise on your own or with a friend or partner with whom

you can feel uninhibited. In both situations you will need:

- a pad of blank paper;
- a pen.

To start refer back to the lists of related yin/yang concepts outlined at the beginning of this chapter. Leave one page for each word. Write each word at the top of the page. For example, page one will be titled receptive, page two: active, page three: earth, etc. If you are working with a partner, lie down in a comfortable, warm place and let him/her interview you. After being given the title of the page you will recite all the ways in which you are receptive, and so on. Your responses should be written down, keeping to the essence of what you are saying. In other words, keep to single words or three- to five-word phrases at the longest for everything you name. With more abstract concepts such as heaven and earth, review their inherent natures and the ways in which you reflect them or say whatever comes to mind when you hear these words and gradually think how you express their qualities practically.

If you decide to do this on your own find a comfortable, warm place where you may sit and write. Go through as many pages as you can in the time you have allowed, taking as many breaks as you require to keep your mind fresh. You may need several sittings to get through both lists.

After You Have Finished

You will have a book that you can always refer to – an energy diary. Look at the lists that are longer. What do they tell you about how you are using your energy? Notice why you are doing these particular activities. Are they arising directly from your interests or are they motivated by other things like guilt or duty? Which areas show balance? Are you happy with this use of energy?

What you see is how you are operating – how you are using your energy. There is no mystery here. When your lists feel complete review them and see if there are any areas you would like to change.

With a different colour ink write the new way next to the old. The next step will be to decide how you get from the old to the new.

Do the inventory every six months to monitor any significant changes.

General Yin Activities

- expression of sadness
- expression of vulnerability
- expression of nurturing
- unconditional love
- feeding oneself and others food and life-supporting information
- self preservation
- organizing family activities
- sensitivity to the feelings of others
- embracing the joy of life
- intuition (trusting in one's sense of what is about to happen)
- warmth
- generosity
- appreciation of nature and beauty

General Yang Activities

- expression of anger
- providing for oneself
- confidence – standing up for oneself and one's convictions
- self-protection
- taking charge/leadership ability
- driving or operating machinery
- cooking
- work with computers and technological equipment
- being physical
- planning ability
- having overall perspective
- getting out of the rut

- lifting oneself by one's bootlaces
- expansion
- adventure
- romance
- instinct (being moved by one's guts)

Neutral Activities (gained from the world)

- music
- art
- ideals
- magnanimity
- justice

Yin from Our Mothers and Yang from Our Fathers

Because of the social conditioning that has split the qualities of yin and yang into gender roles, we can look to our parents' expression of both as keys to the way we relate to yin and yang activities in our lives. In the conditioned response to our yin and yang power we learn to emulate or react to our parents. We learn about the yin or nurturing principle from our mothers, whether biological or guardian, and the yang from our fathers. Consequently, if our mothers were nurturing and giving and enjoyed helping things to grow we either accept or react to these qualities in ourselves. If our mothers did this to the exclusion of their own interests or in a smothering way, we are likely to reject the nurturing principle in ourselves in varying degrees for the purpose of self-preservation.

By the same token, we learn to relate to our yang energies from our fathers. If our fathers terrified us with anger or violence, we would be reluctant to accept the yang power inside and its expression.

Summary of Yin and Yang –
the Fundamental Structure of Power

Everything is composed of yin and yang. They are like the two sides of a coin, like night and day, inside and outside, the boulders and the cascades, the treble and the bass in music. When one force is full and at risk of becoming excessive, it changes into its complement. The Taoist philosophy goes on to explain that when both these forces are in a state of balance the meaning of life or the *tao* is accessible. The meaning of Plato's allegory of the cave is relevant here, too, since unless one is facing life with both eyes open or dancing facing the fire, one's back is turned to the fire and one is left perceiving the mere shadows as reality. The consequences of this imbalance are an inability to direct one's energy over a long period of time, 'burn out', disease, minimized realization and expression of one's potential.

Taking Charge: Balancing Yin and Yang

By balancing the forces of yin and yang in the body through their respective channels – governor and functional, we become increasingly aware of the importance of balancing give with take. The two energies create flow. This dynamic is clearly demonstrated in the wave. One current is rising and moving forward while the other is receding and pulling downward. When pressed into its most essential shape the tao symbol is the wave, the most basic unit of movement, life and vibration.

Music is perhaps the most universal language of yin and yang as it reminds us of the balance of two entities; that we can be inclusive and do more than one thing in any given moment. We can engage both sides of the brain. The harmony of treble and bass transports one-sided thinking into unity.

When we are in balance we create a harmonious atmosphere around us. We are in charge. Energies and ideas which seem divergent are coordinated into action. The charioteer, as is portrayed in the tarot, is an apt illustration with the reins of yin and yang in each hand. Energy is directed effectively towards actualizing our goals. This is power – the effective use of energy.

We have seen how power can be used to hurt or to heal and improve. I stand upon the shoulders of the great spiritual teachers and nuclear physicists who say truth and love are the greatest powers. Destructive forces eventually consume themselves. Power used for the good of all grows. This is the basic principle of the recent martial art of Aikido. Its meaning is the way of love and harmony. One gains more strength from the heart. Truth and love are the substance and binding force of the most basic structural unit, the atom.

Desire – the Motive Behind Power

Consciousness expressed through desire is the bow drawn at a specific degree and aimed at a specific target. Power is the release of the arrow. So it follows that with any given goal we may have, let's say painting or learning a skill, the deeper we feel the desire consciously, the greater the results and the spheres of influence. The drawing, holding and releasing is a useful analogy for describing the three basic dynamic expressions of power: giving – releasing, receiving – drawing, and reserving – holding. These three expressions have other names: yang, yin and tao (the combination of the two).

Giving – releasing
yang – heaven – positive – sun – protective – provisional

Receiving – drawing
yin – moon – negative (though not in a bad or destructive sense) – reflective – intuitive

Reserving – holding
neutral – earth: positive and negative – receptive – nurturing

The Elements: Earth, Air, Fire and Water

Earth Power

How do you express your power? There are a number of possibilities. We will begin with the elements as basic symbols of expression. Practicality is an earthy expression. When we work with our bodies, demonstrate how something is done, write, build, acquire possessions, or manifest, we are using our power in an earthy way. In which ways do you express your earth power?

Air Power

Connecting is the domain of the air. Communication, speaking, different languages, being able to be omnipresent through the mind, putting synthesizing disciplines, reading, breathing, and learning are all airy uses of power. What are the ways in which you express your air power?

Fire Power

Anything to do with play, adventure, romance, passion, enterprise, dance, spontaneity, volatility, inspiration, and creativity comes under the realm of fire power. How do you express your fiery energy?

Water Power

Any form of feeling, sensitivity to others' feelings, letting go, surrendering, merging, dissolving, healing, flowing, moodiness, and sensuality is an expression of water power. How do you express your water power?

States of Mind as Power or Ways of Mobilizing – changing Perspective

Bruce Lee, the famous martial artist, presented a puzzle to his students. He drew a line in the sand and asked: how do you make this line shorter without touching it? He then drew a longer one next to it. I was inspired by this story and added my version which is to move away from the object, person, problem, city, country, etc., and thus diminish its importance. This is true when we go on holiday or vacations. By being in a different setting with different scenery and rules we change our perspective. We broaden it because new input displaces old perspective by stretching it with new information. So in order to return to 'normality' we come back to it with new information, new sensitivity, whether or not we are aware of the new input's influence.

Truth and Love: The Greatest Powers

When all has been levelled the truth of what was is the only remaining edifice.

Love is the force in whose arms we can only blossom.

MAHAL, THE SEER AMONG THEM

She was known for her ability to see through personalities into the souls of those she knew.

When confronted on her naïvety about her strong belief in the healing power of love she listened very quietly, then without warning, opened her mouth and sang Puccini with such feeling that she left them with frozen thoughts, hearts gushing, and begging for more.

Years . . . moments later:
The wind would whisper to her and she began to listen.

4

'PROTECT YOUR POWER INVESTMENT'
the Tool: Chi Maintenance

IS THE 'FORCE' WITH YOU?

How many times have you felt pleasure, a tingling up your spine, the glow in your face, and dismissed it as a good day or a rare, lucky and lovely time? This force of joy and pleasure is the natural way for each of us to feel – all the time. When we are in this state of peace and security we are imbued with our innate vitality. Something that we have done, a way of thinking, a new attitude, a connection we made, a certain atmosphere has put us in touch with our internal nourishing flow: we have tapped our *chi*.

One needn't have been a martial artist for twenty years to experience the effects of chi or one's natural vital energy. It is the integral factor around which the Taoist philosophy revolves as it is the product of the balanced combination of yin and yang which understates its nature. And it is for this reason that the preservation and improvement of chi is at the very root of Chinese medicine. Although the use of chi became recognized academically as a staple in the Taoist philosophical thesis and way of life, its nature is shrouded in the mists of time as chi describes the very force of life. **When you feel the tingles up your spine, when you are inspired and full of joy, when you experience the healthy pinky golden glow you are experiencing chi. The function of chi is to nourish.** The statement 'I can breathe easier in this environment, around this person, in this work setting' is literal and relevant to the mechanism that promotes chi. This is because chi is contacted and circulated when we breathe deeply. We breathe easier when we feel balanced. And although there are universal factors which encourage internal balance such as being around green (the vegetation gives off oxygen) and negative ions (a product of flowing water such as the sea and fountains), each of us has our unique repertoire for building it. Some believe that each of us enters the world with a given amount of chi which is stored in the kidneys, and depending on how we live our lives we either preserve and augment it or gradually diminish it, which results in the degeneration of the mind and body. Breathing in specific ways allows us to touch our greater unlimited selves, the selves that include our bodies but is not limited by them, and improves the circulation of chi. We will explore breathing styles in the next chapter.

The official art for chi cultivation is called Chi Kung which means internal work. There are many approaches to Chi Kung, each has its specific purpose. The people who study this rejuvenating art are equally as diversified. It is for anyone who wishes to improve his/her health and level of inspiration. Chi Kung works to integrate the realms of heaven and earth through the actions of the human. In other words, heaven is the realm of inspiration, earth, the realm of manifestation, and it is through the actions of the human realm, the way we work with our energy, that the two are integrated. This integration reflects the old adage: 'One becomes what one habitually thinks.'

Chi Kung Background

Chi-Kung is the most ancient of the martial arts. It is also a healing technique. Originating in China some 5,000 years ago, this potent method of building reserves of inner strength for effective expression is at the root of Tai Chi Chuan, Kung fu, Karate, and Judo. So powerful was it as a tool for health and fighting strategy that it was kept secret amongst its masters and passed on only to worthy, mature apprentices. Its underlying philosophy has been used for warfare, improving the quality of life, healing people with terminal illnesses, and, within a more modern context, for athletic excellence amongst Olympic candidates and champions. More extraordinary demonstrations of its power include the use of chi to empower one's body to break boards, bricks and stones, heating the body to melt ice, and for withstanding unusual amounts of externally imposed pressure. Its reputation was marred during the Cultural Revolution. It has been slowly regaining its popularity in China and recently in the United States and some parts of Europe.

Fundamentally, Chi Kung involves the use of certain breathing and moving styles (varying from holding a static position to performing intricate dance-like movements) to increase the circulation of the vital energy throughout the body and brain. The techniques develop deep concentration which can be practically translated into developing confidence, competence and productivity. Also, paradoxically, Chi Kung offers a way for athletes and the rest of us to train for speed by slowing down: the often slow pace of the movements taps deep reflexes and facilitates the flow of adrenalin, both necessary for fast reactions. The conditioning of the body and mind which results gives an edge in sports such as tennis, golf, running and rowing, and enhances one's ability to respond quickly and appropriately in a dangerous situation. Chi Kung practitioners frequently report how they have used their skills to avoid accidents in the home or on the roads. The movement sequences provide a backdrop for practitioners to discover and monitor the way they operate in the world and to improve it effectively. This follows the dominant philosophy of Chi Kung which states: 'The way one moves is the way one lives.'

Recognizing Ways in which You Already Practise Chi Kung

On a practical level, we virtually practise Chi Kung when we consciously create and direct our power. Anything that nourishes, inspires and helps us to translate our energy from idea into action is chi enhancing. This includes any activities, work, environments, food, colours, light and heat sources, music, people, places, theories and attitudes. It is natural to feel exhausted after engaging intensely in any activity whether it be mental or physical. However, when we feel chronically tired after participating in any of the above it is an indication that we are being drained rather than enhanced by that activity, person or idea. We are tired when:

1. We are doing something we do not wish to do; we feel trapped.
2. We are letting someone drain us and distract us from whatever is appropriate for us.
3. We are operating in an inappropriate sphere of influence (too grand or too small).
4. We are in the wrong environment or geographical location for a particular stage of our lives.
5. We have outgrown a situation that no longer suits us.

Awareness of draining sources of energy is the first step to moving on. The ancient Taoist text, chapter 33 of the *Tao te Ching* states: 'One who knows others is wise. One who knows oneself is enlightened.'

Before we take a closer look at chi, how it works and its ramifications, let's start with taking stock of how we are already manufacturing chi. We will do this through the following two writing exercises. Habits are difficult to change. The purpose of the writing exercises is to make these more illusive parts of self and habits tangible. Writing anything down is an exercise in integration.

Exercise A   Chi Cultivation and Analysis Chart
In your power notebook write the following topics in columns. Then list all energizing, nourishing areas under each heading.

activities	work	environments	food	colours
walking	*house*	*green*		
swimming	*garden*	*noisy*		
singing	*community*	*work*		
	art			

light	heat sources	water sources	music
candle		the sea	Bach
sun		fountains	Soul II Soul

people	places	theories	attitudes	religions

Exercise B   Sources of Draining Energy

STEP ONE What drains you? Again make headings that suit you. This might include types of actions from people you know, emotions, activities, music, food, environments, etc. Rapidly fill in the space under the titles.

STEP TWO Why do these areas or characteristics drain you? Do you see any possibility of changing these situations in the near future? At another time? When?

These exercises will help you monitor the ways you cultivate or deplete your vitality.

CHI AND ELECTRICITY

Chi is easier felt than seen. However, there are more and more innovative types of photography, for example, ones that register emanations of chi such as kirlian and laser photography. We can also see it in paintings in which halos surround the heads. Chi produces light and therefore maintains some of the characteristics and properties of electricity. Chi and electricity have several aspects in common, the first of which is that they are both unseen energy forces. To perceive them we usually have to look for the effect they have on some other entity.

One way we can perceive the effects of electricity is by turning on a light bulb, en easy task, performed several times a day by most of us. Let's take a moment to think about the complex technology required to enable a light bulb to burn. First, electricity has to be generated, then it has to be trapped in the proper container (wires), and finally it must be transformed into a usable form (a.c., d.c., 220 volts, 110 volts, etc.). And still it isn't of much use until it finds an appropriate mode of expression, such as the filament in a light bulb. There is one more characteristic of electricity that is often overlooked, which is nevertheless quite important – it must be protected. The light bulb's filament will not last very long if it is not surrounded by the right atmosphere and protected by glass.

Now we will see how these five characteristics – generation, storage, transformation, expression, protection – apply to chi.

Generation

Electricity is generated by taking one source of energy, such as fire or running water, and using that power to activate electrical generators.

How is chi generated? There are two ways to activate chi, one uses the body, the other uses the mind. In order to do the movement sequences in Chi Kung, one assumes a special posture where the feet are firmly on the ground, the knees are bent, the body is relaxed yet firmly supported, and there's a feeling of an imaginary string attached to the top of the head which gently stretches the spine upwards. Assuming this posture switches on the chi generator (located a few inches below our navels and a few inches inwards) and allows one to feel the energy already circulating in the body. When we begin to do the movements, they activate the chi. For example, one of the basic exercises involves twisting the waist, and in this particular movement the torso acts like the axle of a wheel; the rim of the wheel is the chi itself. The twisting motion disperses stagnation, and when these forces are dispersed chi can enter. Utilizing different types of breathing also gets the energy moving and opens up the body to allow the chi to flow.

The other way of generating chi is with the mind or the intent. By focusing our minds in certain ways, we switch on the generator; we can then use the mind to project light into different areas, opening them up. Using one's intent is integral to Chi Kung; if the movements are done without the proper intent, they are just empty vessels. This is true with everything we do.

Storage

Like electricity once it is generated, chi needs to be directed to an appropriate container or it will disperse and be wasted. Chi is actually stored in the lower abdomen, in a place called the 'tan-tien'. This highlights another significant way in which an individual receives chi; it is transmitted through the umbilical cord at birth. *Depending upon one's lifestyle, this supply can be depleted, maintained or increased.* This concept is important because one of the results of working with one's chi is to re-establish a connection with the greater energetic umbilical which supplies us with what we need once we have embarked upon our destinies. This is our connection with the inner unified verse – the universe. Nourishment can flow into us through this connection once it is re-established.

In the body, chi is stored in the tan-tien and in certain organs. Meditation, sitting quietly and focusing the mind, is one way to replenish our store of chi. Rest is another way of doing this. When we go to sleep at night we refill our chi reservoir. You can build your chi reservoir by finding time during the day to lie down. In a work situation you might lie in the lounge for three to five minutes on your back with your knees bent if it is more comfortable for your lower back and with the palms of your hands facing the ceiling. Dreaming is another way in which we replenish our chi reserves. By lying down in the manner mentioned above, even for a few minutes, we simulate the sleeping/dreaming processes. In this state information assimilation is expedited. This applies to any learning situation as well. We get better at anything we do not simply through repetitious practice, but because we rest and dream in the interim of those practice times. The dreamlife brings more information to the learning area. Information is shifted to the instinctive and intuitive realms when we rest and is more efficiently integrated. The next time we return to whatever it is we were practising, the thinking energy becomes minimized and automatic efficiency becomes maximized.

Transformation

When electricity is generated it is in a very powerful and amorphous state, and must pass through transformers and be changed into a specific type of current before it is utilized.

When chi is generated and stored in the tan-tien, it is still an undeveloped resource. In order to tap its power and transform it into something useful, we use two basic tools: the use of our bodies and our attitudes. The movements we make stir up the chi and act upon it so that it can be changed into something tangible – something useful. They also enable us to focus the chi and to channel it in various directions. All our movements create a physical structure for the energy; our attitudes create a mental structure and open up certain pathways through which chi can flow. In our lives this is evidenced by the manner in which we work our way around obstacles, or how we can lighten up a particular situation simply by changing our attitude about what is happening. To summarize, all our movements from walking, lifting our cutlery to eat, etc., and our attitude, the way we frame our experiences and later reflect upon them both serve as chi converters.

Expression

According to history books, Benjamin Franklin went out one dark and stormy night to fly a kite. The kite was truck by lightning which travelled down the kite string to a key that was sitting in a jar. Franklin managed to gather a jar full of electricity, but then realized he didn't have an immediate use for it. Humankind had to wait until the light bulb was invented before we could use electricity to light up our lives. Once electricity is generated, it has to have a proper mode of expression or it isn't really of much use to us.

This is true of chi. The way we interact with the world is an expression of our chi. Talking, moving, creating art, working, manifesting our personalities, our life's purpose – these are all manifestations of our most personal light bulbs. This is the way we radiate our life force outwards. To get the desired results, one must direct chi towards an appropriate destination. When we want to utilize electricity we choose which appliance to turn on; when we're cold we turn on the heater, when we want to listen to music we turn on the stereo. It wouldn't make much sense to turn on the stereo and expect it to heat a room. The possible uses for chi are limitless, but one must choose the proper mode of expression to suit one's needs. In an ideal situation one can look back on former modes of expression and realize they were a part of a greater plan.

Protection

This is a very important concept when working with electricity. If the filament in a light bulb is not protected, it will not function properly. If wires are not insulated, they will short out.

In Chi Kung, the key to protection is discrimination, which means being aware of what we let in to which part of us. This has to do with a sense of value – with self-worth. When we value something we are very careful about what we do with it. This care also extends to what is done with it. There is a type of chi called *wei chi*, which is a protective energy that emanates from the mind and body. On a conscious level, it expresses itself as intuition – the ability to sense what is appropriate and what is not, and on an instinctive level, that is, when the body speaks faster than the mind. Such is the case in a dangerous situation when one moves reflexively into safety. On a physical level, wei chi actually strengthens the immune system. It fills up one's energy body so that it is like a spare tyre which, when the body is full of chi, repels detrimental energies; whatever is not useful bounces off. By evaluating ourselves, and doing things to maintain a healthy status, we are actually developing wei chi. This is one of the important effects of monitoring the way we move on a daily basis: when our movements are speedy and jerky this is the way we are living; when they are graceful, no matter what the speed, grounded energy and one's ability to make graceful transitions are indicated.

Perhaps this is a lot to think about. If you are saying to yourself, 'I don't even understand how electricity works, how am I ever going to understand chi?' don't worry. Just as you don't need to be a physicist to plug in an appliance and have it work for you, you don't need to master the concepts behind chi to be able to utilize it. Keep the electricity analogy in mind though, later on it may serve you as a model with which you can identify when and how you are using chi in your life.

CHI AND PERSONAL EVOLUTION

And when placed in a quiet space, the mind, too, becomes quiet and reflects its branches, roots, and all that is anything.

For the moment, let's assume that we have this energy running through us. What good is it? We can't plug a heater into our navel and warm up a room. So besides using chi to strengthen our bodies and immune systems, what exactly is the best use of this nourishing energy? The answer to that question lies entirely within each of us. Chi is our connection with the 'unseen life-force' as Dr Lily Siou a Chi Kung master in Hawaii, describes. Chi, when embraced and developed, can be a great source of power. In Greek mythology, divine power was often symbolized by the gods throwing thunder bolts from their fingertips; this is what it sometimes feels like when surges of chi run through the body and mind. *When chi flows freely through our bodies it is like a gentle breeze singing through a finely tuned instrument*. This feeling, a natural high, comes in a variety of ways. It can begin as a shaking or quaking feeling coming as a result of a chi breaking through physical/emotional blocks, tightness or resistance. This quaking in the body is an indication that we are ready to open to new energies but the old holding pattern asserts its last bit of control. Once we relax with the energy and it begins to flow the shaking subsides. Such is the case when an aeroplane lifts off; once it has defined gravity, made its ascent and reached its designated altitude, the passenger experiences virtual stillness. It is at this time when we upgrade our vibratory rate that we move to another rung of our personal evolutionary spiral. When this happens our understanding expands to larger spheres of influence. We operate with greater facility:

> 'When there is stillness in motion the Tao (a greater reality) appears,' says the ancient Eastern philosophy.
>
> TAOIST PHILOSOPHY

The Notion of Coincidence Is for the Naïve and Irresponsible Mind

Once we recognize that we are in this state of apparent stillness all states of consciousness are in harmony – conscious, unconscious and subconscious. At this time we are highly tuned to our potential, highly charged. Paradoxically, stillness produces speed. This is why some styles of Chi Kung involve movements that are practised very slowly. The slow movements allow the practitioner to go into a dream state while being awake. When this happens the veil between the conscious awake dimension and the unconscious asleep dimension lifts.

I remember having my brainwave patterns monitored by biofeedback equipment. Having done Chi Kung for many years, I was curious about some scientific back-up to something I had suspected for quite a while. I always felt I was dreaming with my eyes open when I performed the slow balletic meditative movement sequences. Shortly into the session, I went from alpha via theta into delta brainwave frequency with high amplitude. This surprised the consultant as theta was the deepest anyone was recorded as going, when a swami was tested at MIT. The consultant couldn't believe I was awake and smiling at him while in a dream state. I told him of my background, mentioning that all of us are capable of doing this when the speed of our movement consciously matches that of our dream state. Several subsequent sessions confirmed this for me.

Keeping still allows us to perceive more of reality than we normally do through the lenses of our personal predicaments, through prejudice and tension. Here movement happens at the deepest level. At this time, one can alter habitual patterns of suffering which leads to the release of the seeds of knowing about how to move on. When these seeds are released and integrated into the life of the practitioner, an evolution into understanding of the greater meaning of life occurs. The pattern of one's destiny is revealed. One becomes more peaceful, more loving, more in tune with the greater flow. Synchronistic events become commonplace. They become witnesses to the fact that one's chi is flowing properly through mind and body and to the bridging that is happening between our inner and outer worlds.

Many of the movements of Chi Kung describe the shape of the spiral. This evolutionary shape speaks of the inherent design of our genetic structure. The double helix of our DNA carries the memory and the know-how of our personal evolution. It is natural for us to grow and we do know how. Pain is sometimes a useful catalyst to our growth:

Pain is the stone which breaks the shell of the fruit.
KAHLIL GIBRAN, FROM *THE PROPHET*

Grief is a natural response to loss. All people have their own timing and way of grieving. Suffering, on the other hand, is either the result of imposed cruelty or a sign that we are holding on to something, an idea, person, place or feeling that is inhibiting our progress. In the case of imposed cruelty, it is the evolutionary work of all of us to transform this way of relating to that of kindness and respect, again, in appropriate and effective ways. When we allow ourselves the stillness while in motion, we feel the movement of our DNA. We evolve at the psychological level when we discover and trust our uniqueness. When we evolve ourselves, we naturally stimulate the memory in others simply by our presence. *Synchronistic events occur, such as thinking something before it happens, singing a song and discovering it on the radio when you turn it on, hoping to meet someone and while you are coming out of a shop they appear. Being in the right place at the right time becomes the norm because it is at this time that we are highly tuned to our potential. One becomes the conduit for and the recipient of unlimited abundance.*

THE 'FORCE' IS IN YOUR HANDS

So how can we recognize we are in this state? How can we know our chi is flowing freely? One way of knowing you are in the flow is through observing the times when your hands are speckled red and white or when they are a bright red colour, as though they are lit up. In the practice of Chi Kung this phenomenon is called 'plum hand'. When the chi is flowing the hands become engorged and feel like the insides of a juicy, ripe plum. This indicates that your chi is flowing through your heart into your hands. Nothing is pulling at your mind, body or heart at this time. Your energy is literally *in your hands*. This is your immediate biofeedback barometer. **It is an excellent time to programme yourself to do the things you may have put off and to initiate confidence to begin new projects, new growth-producing experiences.** When you see your hands expressing the plum state observe your:

1. state of mind;
2. the energy flow in your body;
3. mood;
4. the atmosphere around you.

Which qualities do you find? The following simple exercises can help you achieve this state of being, though please bear in mind that like all the exercises offered in this book it is simply a tool, and is, therefore, subsequent in importance to your actual participation in ways of being that encourage the qualities you've just described.

Exercise

Sit comfortably with your spine upright without being rigid. Rest both hands in your lap. Form a circle with each hand by bringing your thumb and middle finger together. These fingers do not touch. They are about the distance of a thin sheet of paper from each other. Now calm your mind and body, breathe comfortably, and let go in your chest. Imagine a radiant ball of sun in the centre of your chest, warm and radiant. As you feel the warmth circulating open other parts of your body to it, letting it flow through as many parts of you as possible. Once it fills your body, allow it to emanate from all directions of your body as far as you feel connected with it. Let your energy form a three-dimensional spherical halo around you. This is also a source of relaxation and inner peace. Once you tap into this unseen river of energy, it can flow through you like a stream through the forest. This bond with the greater flow has an uplifting effect, one which enables us to find the joy in all areas of life.

Chi and Ki

Many of us think that if such a power does exist, it would certainly require a lifetime of work to manifest even the most elementary results. This is not the case. If your intent is clear and strong, and is pointed in a *potentially fulfilling* direction, results can be obtained the first time you tap into your chi power. Increased pleasure, confidence and productivity are natural effects of working chi. With it, one gains directional strength. The art of Budo or martial arts manifesto states: **'Any action without a potentially fulfilling future is wasted energy and drains one's vitality.'** When one plans one's actions around a harmonious end one is directing chi into the use of *ki*. The concept of ki is Japanese in origin and has the effect of mindfully shaping chi.

Chi and Prana

When one develops the ability to contact and open specific areas of the body and mind with the breath *and* create and surround oneself with a healing atmosphere, one is using a higher expression of chi – *prana*. Prana is chi which is used in coordination with the intent to open and fill space with one's essence, with one's consciousness. Pranic power is used to tap the revelationary force of the chakras, or spiritual/physical/emotional vortices, which relate to specific levels of consciousness in our bodies. It is of East Indian origin and is the fuel which is manufactured and utilized when one practises yoga.

In Figure 5a we can see how the major lines in our hands tell us how we are using our chi. They are Taoist *mudras* or positions of the hands that evoke certain mental, physical and emotional awareness. In the art of Chi Kung analysis these three lines are:

  (i)   the line of longevity;
 (ii)   the line of the spirit;
(iii)   the line of intelligence.

The line of longevity relates to physical constitution and will power. The line of the spirit relates to relationship with a greater, more integrated perspective. The line of intelligence relates to how well you are able to discover your uniqueness and to find successful and fulfilling ways to express it.

Observation of these lines can tell you something about yourself and others. If the lines are faint and not very deep, there is an indication of either a superficial relationship with that particular part of your life, or that you are very sensitive and may not be tapping your deeper resources. The deeper and clearer the lines, the greater the indication of integrated living.

However, we can change these lines and their respective meanings in our lives. The positions of the hands describe both a method for developing these areas as well as the ways in which we can direct energy through various activities to enhance their value. When we

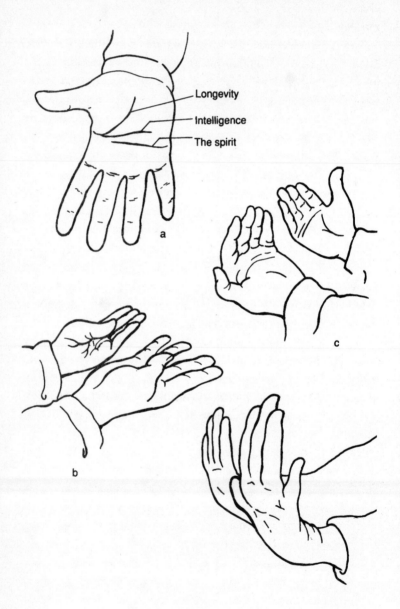

Longevity

Intelligence

The spirit

a

c

b

Figure 5 Chi Kung Analysis

literally furrow or expand these lines by position, we increase the circulation of blood, chi and oxygen to them and to the areas they represent.

Figure 5b shows how we can strengthen our physical constitution by bringing our thumbs inward towards the little fingers. So it follows that any activity you engage in wherein you bring the thumb towards the little finger strengthens your physical constitution, as the thumb has to do with giving ourselves the space to be ourselves and to exerting physical strength with our will power. Doing the washing up, driving, fencing, and horse riding are a few examples.

Figure 5c shows how we can strengthen our perspective or the line of spirit by bringing the four fingers towards the wrists. Any time that we come into ourselves through meditation or yogic types of activities, we strengthen our spirits.

Figure 5d shows how we can strengthen our intelligence by expanding the line. This happens whenever we reach out, make contact with the world or show ourselves. As you increase a balanced repertoire of each of these areas, observe the changes in your lines and their related areas. Do this every six months.

See how your hands contain maps of your chi. Realize little by little how the force is in your hands. Watch your energy level and concentration improve. Feel your ability to get things done expand into challenging areas. Galvanize your power to take your life into your hands – to go where you want to and do what you really want to do!

5

CHI CYBERNETICS: A WAY OF RECYCLING NATURAL ENERGY THROUGH THE BODY
Therapeutic Exercises for Instigating Change

There is a branch of science called cybernetics which deals with our relationship to machines. Specifically, cybernetics explores the similarities and differences between the structure and function of computers and that of the human brain. The knowledge gathered from this discipline enables us to build more efficient machines.

The facet of Chi Kung which deals with the relationship between human beings and nature extends into yet another potent realm of possibilities. I call this branch of science Chi cybernetics. By comparing the structure and function of humans with that of other natural phenomena, we increase our understanding of both ourselves and nature. If used properly, this understanding enables us to build and empower more natural, potent and fulfilled human beings.

Jung discusses the machine/man/nature conflict in *Man and His Symbols* (Arkana, 1990):

Our intellect has created a new world that dominates nature, and has populated it with monstrous machines . . . Man is bound to follow the adventurous promptings of his scientific and inventive mind and to admire himself for his splendid achievements. At the same time, his genius shows the uncanny tendency to invent things that become more and more dangerous, because they represent better and better means for wholesale suicide.

In view of the rapidly increasing avalanche of world population, we have already begun to seek ways and means of keeping the rising flood at bay. But nature may anticipate all our attempts by turning against man his own creative mind. The H-bomb, for instance, would put an effective stop to overpopulation. In spite of our proud domination of nature, we are still her victims, for we have not even learned to control our own nature.

In the preceding paragraph Jung says we dominate nature, and yet we are her victims. Which statement is true? Perhaps both, perhaps neither. The truth of the matter is that we're not quite sure what is going on between us and nature, between us and machines. But we are catching on to the fact that we'd better improve our understanding in this area pretty soon, because we are manufacturing machines that can wipe out the entire planet, and we are altering nature in ways that seem to be leading to our own destruction. These ideas have been clearly demonstrated to us by the fact that the deforestation of remote jungles is affecting the weather patterns all over the Earth. We are gradually realizing that when a tree falls in the forest, any forest, it does indeed affect the lives of all of us on Earth. If the existence of a tree in the Amazon has a direct effect on my life, doesn't it make sense to postulate that my presence on Earth in turn has an impact on this tree with which I will never even come into contact? If my existence has an impact on everyone and everything on Earth, perhaps I'd better try to gain more understanding of how I fit into the whole scheme of things. Chi cybernetics is one way to do this.

In our quest to understand or 'control' nature, perhaps we could take Jung's advice and learn to understand and control our own nature first. The five exercises presented in this section are all designed to increase our perceptions of ourselves as natural entities. Along with this perception comes a better understanding of ourselves and our environment, and through this understanding we gain the ability to act upon the natural forces in our lives, thereby creating change.

Recycling stress is one way to cope with an energy that has been translated into uncomfortable pressure in our bodies. With this attitude and its daily practice we can open to a larger context, one which allows us to feel our place in a larger scheme. *At first this awareness will be mental with some emotional connection. Cultivated over time and with strong intention, our bodies will become inbued with the expanded joyous sensation that is the result of 'opening up' or feeling connected and supported by the larger scheme. This is being grounded in its deepest sense. At this time space and time are expanded as is the sense of more energy, choices and personal power.*

Another message to be understood from all this is that each person on the face of the Earth has the power to change the course of human development. What you do matters. *The choices we make affect the planet in ways we haven't yet begun to understand.*

PREPARATORY WORK FOR CHI CYBERNETICS

Mental Preparation

We have already discussed in the previous chapter the importance of intent in Chi Kung training, together with the importance of grounding and centring in the introduction. Now I will show how; but before we do that a few introductory remarks are necessary.

The practice of centring, through focusing one's attention on the area between the naval and the top of the pelvis, is perhaps the most important preparatory/maintenance exercise in the vast array of Chi Kung styles. And it is this dual-purpose function that makes it particularly critical for this integrated style. I am referring to sinking the mind to the tan-tien (lower abdomen). Once fully grasped, it is the most practical and has the most lasting impact. Before movement begins and after it ends its centring and integrative effects linger.

You will be able to master the forms and therapeutic exercises and all the meditations with this as your foundation. *Also, it is through this concept/exercise that disabled people are enabled to practise Chi Kung effectively.*

Many modern Western people identify themselves primarily with the head with the body lagging subjectively behind. Let's embrace this fact and begin to explore how it can work for you.

1. Tune into your head. What's happening there?
2. Now tune into the centre of your head. What's happening there?
3. Now tune into the back of your head. What's happening there?

This is meant to give you a sample of how ironically out of touch we are with our own heads. Each of these different spaces is a room with specific resources in which your awareness and, later, consciousness may live. Each of these areas contains relevant information about the past, present and future. Much of our disadvantage, we rarely tap these resources because so much of our awareness is focused in the frontal region where we do our rationalizing, thinking, worrying, calculating and survival-orientated mental activity. Sometimes this use of mental space is referred to as intellect, thinking – lower mind. There is another mind that contains infinite access to all forms of information – the enlightened intuitive, higher mind, the one referred to earlier as using expanded awareness.

In order to access the power of the higher intuitive mind, you must sink the lower mind to the tan-tien. Here it can rest, relax and act instinctively as a supportive protective agent to the higher mind. The thinking mind, when emanating from this place, can truly activate the higher mind's power, and hence reach its own potential. This, of course, has implications in the conscious development of personal power.

Just as the river bed provides space and support for the flow of the river so does the sunken, centred mind support and create space for the flow of the higher mind – the grounded and intuitive, spontaneous mind.

Mind to Tan-Tien Exercise

Begin by standing or sitting comfortably. Notice how you feel. What is your mood. What are you thinking about? If standing, have your feet shoulder width apart. Bring your hands to your lower abdomen with the left hand covering the right. Make sure that the inner knuckles of the left hand cover connect with the outer knuckles of the right hand. Connect the tip of your tongue to the roof of your mouth. These two connections will automatically connect the yin/yang energies and starts the chi flow. Breathe in a natural comfortable manner.

Now bring your awareness to your head. Without judgement notice what is happening there. Put that activity on an imaginary lift and imagine it slowly going down through your throat, chest, solar plexus, abdomen, and finally to your lower abdomen where it settles into the dome-shaped floor of your tan-tien. Notice what is happening in that area . . . to your hands and to your feet.

This grounds the mind and body so that the chi may proceed along its instinctive cleansing, healing, empowering path.

Once you feel comfortable with the effects of the thinking mind's new residence here, split your awareness and go back up to your head. What's it like in there now? Having made this observation, how do you feel, emotionally, physically, mentally?

This exercise has escorted you into your inner world and simply through the act of observation in these key areas, you have effected change.

Unravelling Identity

Sun–Moon Centres

In the practice of Chi Kung, observations without judgement is a major goal. Initially, this is retrospective as in the case of a practitioner realizing that present-life circumstances are a result of previous awareness and points of interest, or an awareness of the effects of a movement sequence hours or days later. As more understanding occurs this understanding becomes increasingly immediate. One is always striving to get a more conscious understanding of what is going on inside – what are the inherent compositions of the self, what motivates us into specific actions?

The thinking mind in tan-tien exercise works with the dynamic interplay between sun–moon energies. The sun discussed here is a centralized conduit of yang forces in the mind/body/emotion paradigm. It is located at the root of the navel. The heart acts on the amalgamation of impulses from the sun centre. Just as in our solar system it is pure awareness and radiates outward. *Sun is to do with pure uninhibited expression. It is associated with the right side of the body. Related qualities include protective nature, fiery impulses, intellectual processes, consciousness, heat and expansion.*

And as in the solar system the moon reflects the light of the sun, so also does the moon force represent a centralized conduit of the yin energies. It is located in the upper centre of the head (the base at eyebrow level; the top touches the inner side of the crown). The moon is associated with receptivity, intuition and the right side of the body. Other related qualities of the moon include watery impulses, the colour white, coldness, contraction and wisdom.

Allow yourself to feel your personal interpretation of these two centres, first separately and then simultaneously. What other qualities can you add to both lists? Through the acknowledgement of these two centres you may begin to clarify the source of your motivations.

Breathing

The importance of breathing is emphasized in most physical activities such as exercise, yoga, martial arts, swimming and other sports. Chi Kung is often viewed first and foremost as a method of breathing. With all the different variations, it is no wonder that so many people are overwhelmed as to which form is appropriate for them and for what purpose.

First, let's look at the major styles of breathing and grasp their purpose. The breath is meant to be the vehicle of *shen* or spirit. The initial purpose of breathing is to break the limited thinking cycle or 'being, in one's head' and shifts the focus back to the body and its natural rhythms. This takes one out of the fight–flight mode and allows a return to simply being. When one is in this state of 'simply being' you are in a high potential state. I like to think of it as being in charge of both energy channels, yin and yang – positive and negative being in harmony. Such is the case in the zen breathing where one is instructed to count ten breaths. Once this is mastered, excessive focus on one's breath can actually distract from awareness and later, consciousness.

It is at this stage that it is crucial for one to allow the breathing to be automatic and to use it as a springboard into following shen (spirit). This is the highest state of Chi Kung practice as it implies a total flow with one's spontaneous higher mind.

There are three major categories of breathing:

1. Physical – the most natural thing we do.
2. Mental – way of infusing life into ideas to give them substance.
3. Spiritual – way of breathing the universe through self (inhale heavenly inspiration; exhale earthly manifestation).

Buddhist Breathing Style

Inhale into the lower abdomen, including the lower back, filling it like a tyre expanding. This is for the purpose of grounding and relaxing visceral organs, especially the intestines, liver, spleen, stomach. Each inhalation infuses these organs with chi which increases the circulation of blood and oxygen in those organs.

Taoist Immortal Breathing or Reversed Breathing

Inhale into the upper chest while drawing in the abdomen. Release the abdomen and exhale gradually down through the pelvis, legs and feet. This style of breathing helps to develop a higher perspective. It forces one to breathe into the energy vortices (chakras) of higher awareness (the heart chakra, throat, third eye and crown). Breathing into these higher regions raises one's vibration, creating more energy in the body and hence increases one's potential for consciousness and manifestation. Exhaling down into the feet enables one to ground this energy and feel the body as a safe vessel/vehicle for it.

THE BODY PUMP
INTRODUCED BY

The Fable of Ten-year Butterfly

In the Himalayas there is a species of butterfly that is rather unusual. While all the other species hatch every spring, this particular type tends to emerge only once in a decade. The people there have a fable which explains this phenomenon.

It seems that the ten-year butterfly begins life as a very happy caterpillar. It eats a great deal, thoroughly enjoying what it eats. It crawls around on the ground and likes the feel of the earth beneath its many feet. It feels warm and safe inside its furry body. When the time comes for it to make a cocoon, it makes a particularly strong one so that it will continue to feel warm and safe as it hibernates.

In fact, it feels so much at home inside the cocoon that when spring comes and all the other caterpillars hatch into butterflies, it decides to remain as it is for another year. When its friends come round singing sweet songs of life, telling how wonderful it is to have wings and soar upon the breeze, it remembers how much it enjoyed crawling upon the earth, and adds another layer of silk to its cocoon so that it may go back to sleep and immerse itself in memories for another year.

When the next spring rolls around and the caterpillar once again hears the butterflies revelling in life, it gives some thought to the idea of joining them, but flying seems like a dangerous thing to do, so the caterpillar fortifies its cocoon and safely sleeps again.

The next spring, the caterpillar hears more about the beauty and glory that it will experience when it emerges. But it realizes that it is hearing these things from the grandchildren of the caterpillars who were its friends when it went into hibernation. Death seems like too high a price to pay for being a butterfly, so the caterpillar adds another layer to its hiding place, to keep death at bay.

By the fourth year, memories of living on the earth have begun to fade, and they are replaced by splendid dreams of flying free. But still the caterpillar is not ready to abandon its familiar sanctuary, so it dreams away another year.

When the fifth spring comes, the ten-year butterfly can barely hear the joyous songs of life through the thick walls of its cocoon. It decides that it had better emerge before it is too late. But by now it is trapped in an imposing edifice which has hardened over the years. So, naturally, it takes the ten-year butterfly five years to undo what it took five years to build.

After ten years, it finally emerges, but the long ordeal has faded its beauty and sapped its strength. It does not fly as high as the other butterflies, nor live as long, yet it sings the song of life just as sweetly.

Before you read the rest of this chapter, take a moment to ask yourself this question: 'What is confining me, what are the threads of my cocoon made of?'

> *Listen more often to things than to beings.*
> SWEET HONEY IN THE ROCKS, *BREATHS*

Introduction

This exercise will invigorate you by transmuting stagnant energy in the body and brain. As a result you experience an increased level of energy, directional strength and productivity. Having these qualities at your disposal will enable you to move through life's transitions more gracefully – an invaluable survival tool. Harmony is the key outcome here – harmony between conflicting parts of yourself such as mind and emotions, career and family, strengths and limitations. From this internal harmony a continuity with external factors will develop. It becomes much easier to blend with nature and other people, and to integrate ancient information into a modern context.

Preparation

a. *Stance:* Set the solid foundation! Stand with legs slightly wider than shoulder-width apart. Make sure the power base of your pelvis is secure under your shoulders with the tip of your spine pointing downwards towards the centre of the Earth. Your knees should be comfortably bent to facilitate a springy quality from the top of your pelvis down through the legs. The body should be relaxed and open so that energy can flow freely.

b. Now be sure that the tip of your tongue touches the roof of your mouth to unite the yin/yang channels of the microcosmic orbit. Allow the tip of your tongue to rest comfortably behind your upper teeth.

Technique

1. Sensitize first the tops and then the undersides of your arms, especially your wrists, as they will be the leading segment of your arms in this technique.

2. After you have effectively sensitized these areas by focusing your awareness on them, raise your wrists in front of you to shoulder level *and no higher*. (Raising your arms higher will disconnect you from the power of your tan-tien.) Initiate the movement from your lower tan-tien. Feel the fullness of this movement as a wave at full crest. This is the upward swing. It pulls the energy up the backs of your legs along your spine to the top of your head. Hold the fullness for three seconds initially, creating a suspension effect before going to the next half of the technique. The suspension time (quiet time) is of utmost importance in movement meditation sequences, because it is within this expression of intention that the chi flows in, bringing insight and illumination.

3. Allow the fullness of the upward swing to be the initiating point of the next motion: the downwards and back swing. The downwards swing allows the chi to cascade down the front of your body, flushing out stagnant energy and sending it into the Earth. To achieve this next part allow the sensitivity of the underside of the forearms to lead you. Go as far behind your back as you can (without strain) and as high up. The higher up you raise your

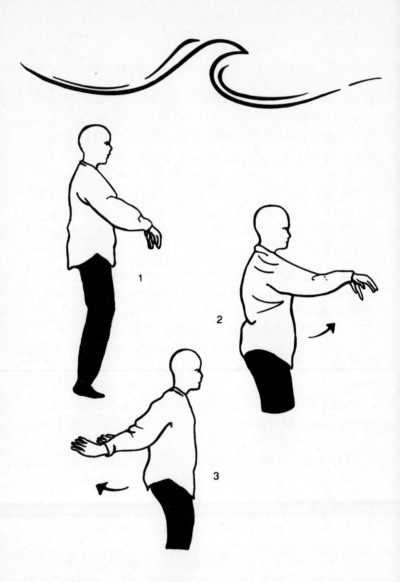

Figure 6 The Pump

arms, the more elasticity you will give to your pectoral region, back and shoulders. (This is a very important area. It is the foundation for projecting your love and creativity out into the world, much as the strength and elasticity of the legs are bioenergetically supportive of creating an inner climate of connectedness and confidence – see *Stand Your Ground*, chapter 6.)

4. *The upward-downward swing combination:* The technique follows the energetic motions of activating a bicycle pump, i.e. as you raise your arms there is a light feeling with a slight resistance from below, as happens when you raise the piston of a bicycle pump. When you initiate the downward swing there is the feeling of moving through pressure, similar to pressing the piston of the pump down.

Do this nine times very slowly or until you feel comfortable with the technique and feel energy moving in your body. Then increase the speed progressively so that you do a total of ninety-nine in one minute. When you have achieved this, slow down with five more. Count 1 . . . 2 . . . 3 . . . 4 . . . 5 and let each succeeding motion be slower than the previous one, and on five trace a large circle (in an outward motion using the blades of your arms and hands) with your arms in front of you.

This circular motion puts a tidy conclusion to the exercise and allows you to make a smooth transition into the next technique.

Knowledge
This exercise enables you to experience the flow of energy within your body as if it were a wave. Waves are created by opposing forces acting upon the same entity. Celestial attraction and water currents force the ocean upwards, and Earth's gravity brings it crashing back down. In the course of our daily lives, we are faced with a myriad of opposing factions. We are constantly making decisions, choosing options. How we respond to this chaos of opposing forces creates the flow of our days.

The ocean has its own rhythm just as your body does. Feelings of expansion/contraction, tension/relaxation, and filling/emptying are often experienced internally as the body pump is being performed. The expansion/contraction feeling of the body pump is an expression of space: expansion opens up space, contraction shrinks it. Although we are not always conscious of it, expansion and contraction are going on constantly in our bodies. Our hearts and lungs experience this dynamic with each breath, each heartbeat.

On an attitudinal level this relates to how we perceive possibilities in our lives. Have you ever had a day when you felt very closed off, as if almost every facet of your life was somehow stagnant and unsatisfying, and it seemed as if there was very little likelihood that things would ever change? Then, just a few days later everything seems to have opened up, the world seems brighter, the possibility for change is right there in front of you. Some people look upon a piece of paper as just an empty sheet. Others see it as a wealth of possibilities: a poem to be written, a picture not yet drawn, a paper aeroplane to be flown. *If you feel an emptiness in your heart, a blank space in your mind, this might just be an expression of possibilities not yet realized.*

Tension and relaxation are two facets of the pump energy which we perceive fairly easily with our five senses. When stress levels rise, our muscles contract, our bodies become tense. Levels of tension and relaxation in our bodies can be direct indicators of how much stress and pressure we are experiencing in our lives. In this way, tension functions like our own personal biofeedback machine. An individual's blood pressure is often an accurate indicator of how much emotional strain that person is experiencing at the time. **Reducing the amount of stress in our lives tends to reduce the amount of tension in our bodies. It is likely that the inverse of this statement is also true, and that by relaxing our bodies we reduce the amount of stress in our lives.**

Filling/emptying is related to expansion/contraction. When something expands, it creates a space to be filled. The heart fills with blood, the lungs take in air, the mind gets crammed with thoughts and ideas. Once something is full, it can only stay that way as long as no fresh input is required. In the cyclical system, fullness is followed by a pause and then the emptying process begins, creating space for a new influx. This process has a lot to do with timing. Everything requires a certain amount of time to become 'full'. As a matter of fact, we tend to measure time by observing the fullness/emptyness cycles in nature. The lunar calendar is based upon the waxing and waning of the moon. Twice a year, on the equinoxes, the days and nights are equal in length, the rest of the time they are either growing shorter (emptying) or becoming longer (filling).

Timing can figure prominently in a person's success in any given endeavour. How many times have you heard someone explain a missed opportunity by saying 'I was in the right place at the wrong time'? And how often do we chalk up a social blunder to 'bad timing'? The truth of the matter is, success doesn't always hinge upon 'who, what, where, how,' or even 'how much'. Sometimes it's a question of 'when'. An improved understanding of natural rhythms helps us to know 'when the time is ripe'. Flowing waters collect no useless material.

Having experienced the reality of the concepts and the effects of the pump technique, you are now equipped to integrate its value – its meaning. It is at this level that you improve the quality of your life.

I remember my grandmother constantly reciting the following verse from the Bible: 'Wisdom is the principal thing. Therefore, get wisdom and in all your getting, get an understanding' (Proverbs 4:7). This verse remained a puzzle to me until I worked with the pump. What could be *more* worth 'getting' than wisdom, I wondered? The pump showed me that there is a difference between 'knowing' and 'understanding'. The pump is about taking something in, changing it, and then putting it out. We take in knowledge, and it mixes with what's already inside us. This blending can sometimes produce a by-product called wisdom. When we base our actions upon the wisdom inside us, then we show that we do indeed 'understand'.

When we actively tune in and feel the sensation of our heart pumping, we are connected with our feet, our heads, and the pulse of all humanity. And even though our hearts may beat at different rates, the fact that they are all indeed beating establishes common ground. From this platform of common ground we may delve deeper to feel our connection with nature – with all living things, animate and inanimate. This delving attitude affords us sensitivity to the forces of life which resonate at different unique rhythms within each individual entity. At this level we hear the symphony of life.

The body pump is progressive in its nature, and this progressive theme is eloquently stated in Kahlil Gibran's love letter to Mary Haskell.

[New York]

Beloved Mary, Thursday, January 28, 1915

I have been asleep during the past three weeks. I have thought of a thousand things which I must do this year. I fear, Mary, that I shall never be able to realize my dreams fully. I always fall short. I always get a shadow of the thing I want.

It used to give me pleasure to hear people praising my work – but now I am strangely saddened by praise, because praise reminds me of things not yet done – and somehow I want to be loved for what I have not done yet. I know this sounds rather childish, but how can one help wanting what one wants? Last night I said to myself, 'The physical consciousness of a plant is not directed towards the past summer but toward the coming spring. The physical memory of a plant is not that of days that are *no more* but of days *that will be*. If plants are certain of a coming spring, through which they will come out of themselves, why cannot I, a human plant, be certain of a spring to come, in which I will be able to fulfill myself?'

Perhaps our spring is not in this life, Mary. This life may be nothing but a winter.

Beloved Prophet: The Love Letters of Kahlil Gibran and
Mary Haskell and Her Journal, edited by V. Hilu, 1972.

If repeated emotional cycles are a source of agony in your life, then you can use the body pump as a tool to help you reshape your psyche. The pump allows you to wash stagnant energy down into the earth where it can become compost and then be drawn back into the body, bringing with it new insight and new information. In this way we can recycle energy that has been translated into stress in our bodies. Some call this transmutation the path to enlightenment. Our purpose here is certainly to open space and shed light on problematic areas. At first, this awareness will be mental, with some emotional content. But by cultivating the wave feeling over time, with strong intention behind it, our bodies will become imbued with the expanded joyous sensation that is the result of 'opening up' and feeling connected to and supported by the larger scheme. This is being grounded in its deepest sense. At this point, space and time are expanded and we feel as if we have more energy, more choices, and increased personal power. Events that once may have seemed coincidental blend more meaningfully to give us insight into the greater whole. Your magnetic power will increase and draw to you the things which are necessary and consistent with your essence. At this point, we become the 'changer and the changed', the phrase that songwriter/visionary Chris Williamson uses in her song 'Waterfall'.

Another side-effect of this technique is that once the individual has experienced this interconnectedness with the environment, he realizes that he has the power to change the course of human development. Each tree, each flower, each person, affects the web of life in ways we haven't yet begun to understand. Jung says: 'As any change must begin somewhere, it is the single individual who will experience it and carry it through. The change must indeed begin with an individual; it might be any one of us' (*Man and His Symbols*, p. 91).

To illustrate how the body pump can affect an individual's life, I would like to share with you some of the experiences and feelings I have had while writing this chapter. As I have been writing about the body pump, my life seems to have filled with unexpected love and support from family, friends and even my pet cats and goldfish. There

seems to be lovely rapport, a harmonious feeling, mutual appreciation and uplifting communication. I feel closer to people, more sensitive to their needs and they to mine. As I was writing the phrase
'coming home', Dvorak's New World Symphony came on the radio.
The melodic theme has been simplified into a single song called
'Coming Home'. Many other synchronistic events have coloured
my week as well. Typifying the flow, synchronicity is a magical characteristic by-product of the Pump. The quality of my life at this
moment feels very high. I have this feeling generally after doing the
Pump, yet, somehow, writing about it has heighted and deepened
the pleasurable effect.

A student of mine recently told me that since she has been doing
Chi cybernetics, she has experienced a marked improvement in her
ability to do her job. She said that for the duration of her work as a
secretary she had felt somewhat overwhelmed by the many tasks
required of her. They seemed disjointed – completely unrelated.
After doing the Pump she noticed herself flowing through the tasks.
They all seemed related and easy. She could spend a given amount of
time on one task and not feel rushed to get to the next. There seemed
to be more hours in each working day, and this took a tremendous
amount of pressure off her because she knew she'd have plenty of
time to get everything done.

Summary

Essentially the Pump will connect you with your instincts. You will
be able to empower yourself with the pump when you need to 'get to
the heart of the matter'. Use it when you are feeling stuck and need
to dissolve rigid boundaries. The energetic pattern of the Pump, the
wave, washes away the boundaries that limit us and keep us separ-
ate from useful parts of ourselves, our environments, other people,
and the secrets of the universe.

When you pump energy through your body you are drawing it up
from the Earth through your feet, swirling it around in your body,
emotions and brain, and projecting it out as energetic matter into
the future. You are, in essence, creating the future. The effects of

these techniques are cumulative as well as immediate. Each time you do the Pump you are adding to your energetic investment account. The Pump creates a state of mind – one which draws in necessary information and propels you into taking action. It propels you into making decisions rather than brooding over problematic areas. It encourages you to be more productive in a relaxed manner, and to detach yourself from the uncomfortable clutches of bureaucracy. The wave provides energy and insight to carry on in the face of obstacles.

The wave is the current that connects us with the greater flow. Your participation in this technique adds to the momentum of the greater flow. By incorporating the wave you have effectively created more unity within yourself and in your environment.

Let yourself go! Become the wave. Open to the love and support that is waiting for you.

THE FOUNTAIN

Which fears are you ready to release into
expressing the greater you?

It is the disease of not listening that I am most troubled with.
WILLIAM SHAKESPEARE

The Fountain refers to four things:

1. an ability to bring that which is within, out into the public domain;
2. the ability to recycle any given amount of energy; and, as a result of this recycling,
3. to tap an apparently endless supply of energy; rejuvenation, hence the fountain of youth;
4. to join forces with a different personality type, a different element, and to flow with the intent of that different point of

view; then to return to one's own perspective enriched with more information.

Successful communication is the purpose of the Fountain and results when we listen deeply to ourselves and to the hearts of others, sharing our energy with them. This energetic exchange also extends to places, animal and things. Whenever we are communicating, hearing the other person's intent and making known ours, we are exercising the Fountain. Communication comes in many forms and is sometimes effectived in ways that are foreign to us.

Practising the Fountain Physically

The Fountain progresses from the pump and this is the purpose of the tidy ending of the previous exercise. After you have learned the Fountain as a physical exercise you may progress smoothly into it.

Step One: The stance: get into the stance described for the Pump.

Step Two: The hands

1. Turn the backs of your hands towards each other.
2. Raise both wrists up to chin level and then open and spread your hands so each finger extends like a ray of sun.
3. Keeping your elbows at a forty-five degree angle to your sides, and your fingers spread apart, continue to move your hands in a fanlike motion out to the sides.
4. When your hands are up and just to the outsides of your body at a forty-five degree angle press downward below your hips until your shoulders and chest relax.
5. Pause for a moment or until you feel still and quiet inside.
6. Begin again and repeat nine times.
7. Reflect upon the meaning of the Pump to prepare yourself for relating harmoniously in the human realm.

Figure 7 The Fountain

I'd like to share six examples from my personal memoirs in which I had to switch languages to communicate:

Bridging the Language Barrier

1. Teaching in Mexico

Body Language

Eleven years ago I was in Mexico teaching self-defence to some university students. My Spanish is minimal to say the least, and the students didn't speak any English, so we had two interpreters in the hope of bridging our language differences. Everything I talked about had a physical technique to demonstrate the message. Shortly into the course, the students told the interpreters they were not needed. I was speaking English, they Spanish, and the communication was higher than in any of my American classes. Body language, their interest and empathy with the topic, and the strong intent to overcome the language barrier, won over our cultural differences.

Sometimes we listen harder to people with foreign accents.

2. Teaching Teen Girl Gangs

Costume, Props and Verbal Language

Another experience comes to mind of a time when I was asked to work in the area of self-esteem, with two gangs of girls who were searching for their identity in violence towards each other. The violence took place primarily in the rest rooms at school. One incident had left one girl nearly blind from stab wounds. At the time, I responded to any request as an opportunity to share and improve my skills. This was to be a two-day course.

DAY ONE When I arrived I knew I had a challenge ahead of me when all of them turned their backs on me as I was about to speak. The communication deteriorated steadily from then on. Without an ounce of success I went home in tears. However, committed to these two days, I pulled myself together and realized I would have to speak their language to make any progress. I remembered their uniform – torn jeans and scarves around their heads. I also lucidly recalled the popular reggae music they played on their 'ghetto blasters'. This was another of the many ways they blocked what I was attempting to say. Then there was their communication with each other: swearing was the dominant speech of the day. So I decided to align and arm myself with their tactics, much to the chagrin of my normal mild-mannered, serene nature.

DAY TWO With borrowed worn and torn jeans, scarf wrapped and tightly tied around my head my personal 'ghetto blaster' blaring slightly louder than the sum of theirs, and a mouthful of language that would 'make the sailors blush', I entered the venue full of emotion and swearing at the top of my voice about the awful state of the f——in' world, and continued until they stood, quiet and astonished – this time facing me. Then seizing the moment with great rapacity, I rudely invited one of the leaders to help me demonstrate a physical technique. 'Hey you,' I shouted, 'get over here and help me.' The leader of the other team sniggered arrogantly so I sent her out to fetch me a glass of water. She did, in a huff, of course. This command left the rest of them stunned. From then on it was plain sailing. Mission accomplished.

Here was an example of finding a practical way to communicate with people whose backgrounds and modes of expression appeared to be grossly different from mine. I used the philosophy, if you can't beat them, join them. I had to work a bit harder by stretching my personality to meet the occasion and dig deep into myself and find courage to *become them*. Imitation would have been inflammatory to the situation. This was a natural high for me as getting through to them far outweighed my bruised ego of day one.

Six months later I rang the school to find out how they were doing. Most of them had channelled their aggression into sports. Two of the girls had decided to go to fashion school in addition to improving their grades in school. There had been no further incidences of violence. This is another example of relating the Fountain.

Cutting through Terrorism

3. Little Boy

Empathy and Matching Anger

One of my most treasured working experiences was at a Toddler Care Centre in Santa Cruz, California where I had three functions – I washed loads of nappies, was a custodian and a part-time toddler carer. Admittedly, this was an excellent harbour for me to reconnect vicariously with the child inside me. The story is about a precious event that occurred in the carer department.

In this centre the children were treated with a lot of respect. Their needs came first and foremost. There was one little boy, however, who was respected by other toddlers and carers alike for a different reason. He was built like a little tank and was very strong for his age. Putting it mildly – he was a terror! He would run round biting, hitting, kicking and pulling the hair of the other toddlers. Whenever meals were served he would grab food from the others' plates and throw it at them and at the carers. When it was time to change his nappy he was at his most ferocious. All the carers would look at each other in the hope that one of them would volunteer for this very unpleasant task. Most of the time I worked as a carer I was on playground duty, so I felt lucky to be absolved of the domestic duties.

One day he was in peak terrorist form. He had missed two changing sessions as no one was willing to receive the brunt of his wrath. So guess what? They invited me to have a go. I was just as terrified as they were. In my attempt to summon the forces to help, I remembered that James seemed particularly cantankerous before and after his nappy change. This, I took to be a clue to what upset him. So with a deep breath and a comical crossing of myself, I entered the lion's den. As I approached him he began with his ritual of kicking. I backed away and in that moment looked at his face. It was blood red with fury. Beneath his gravely furrowed brow he was gritting his teeth. This behaviour was no great mystery. I recognized these expressions as characteristic of anger. Actually, I was rather angry because one of his kicks landed in a vulnerable spot on my torso. My anger gave me a head start to what I was to do next.

In a very loud voice I screamed, 'It really pisses you off that you can't help change your nappy, doesn't it?'

At that moment the mask was removed. James stopped kicking, gritting his teeth, etc. It was apparent to me that the anger and helplessness he must have been feeling for a long time had expressed itself as a toddler/carer terrorism. No one had listened to what was really going on.

'Would you like to help with the change of your nappy?' I asked. He nodded. 'Well, you can. *You* may look at your nappy when I remove to see what you've done. *You* may wipe yourself with the warm flannel. *You* may sprinkle on the powder to prevent nappy rash is, and, finally *you* may spread the powder on yourself. However, there are certain things that I will be in charge of and will not ask for your help. I will put your nappy in the nappy pail. I will run the hot water from the tap to wet the clean-up flannel. I will lift you to put your nappy under you and I will pin the ends of it together. Do you understand?' Again, he nodded yes. We proceeded harmoniously with each step. We maintained eye contact the whole time and he had a big smile on his face.

Finally, he had been heard. He had wanted to know what was going on and to participate in this very personal and important activity. He had felt powerless and left out with no sense of boundaries because everyone was afraid of him. His stifled creative expression had been diverted into his search and destroy manoeuvres. When I communicated with him with respect as an intelligent person, he responded. All of us respond to this kind of treatment, so do animals and insects.

4. *Are You the Cause or the Effect of Your Interactions?*

The Case of the Over Protective Mother
I have found that when we accuse someone of being over protective or defensive, we are actually not taking responsibility for the way we

approached them, or we interacted in such a way as to encourage this type of response. Perhaps they had recently been hurt and we were touching a sensitive nerve. In the Fountain, the energy that we emit comes back to us: we reap what we sow. Karma, and cause and effect and two ways of coming to terms with this energetic exchange. Sometimes this is direct as when we do something to others and then someone does it to us. At other times it is not so cut and dried, as when unpleasant things happen to us when we weren't doing anything to hurt others.

An example of this was a little boy whose mother rang for a consultation because her 8 year-old son was being bullied daily. I couldn't quite understand it because he was blond, blue-eyed and of average skill level. It obviously wasn't racial attack. After three sessions we discovered that his mother was the only parent and very overprotective as a result. I also found, in the way I observed her interact with him, that she rarely gave him a chance to speak. Her domineering approach left him little room to express himself. She always 'knew what was best for him'. In the previous two sessions, I had worked with him using physical self-defence skills and found that under his timid, shy veneer was a very physical and powerful little boy. I also worked with him with handpaints and observed an obvious sense of beauty and form. I deduced that the oppression he was experiencing at school, through the bullying and beatings, was a reflection of what was happening to him in his relationship with his mother at home. He was being suppressed.

Sometimes life has a way of exaggerating relationships with ourselves by bringing it home to us in our relationships with others. After I had reflected his talents back to him and he felt in command of them, he carried himself in a more upright and confident manner. The bullying seemed to stop suddenly. His self-worth was restored. The energetic pattern of the internal suppression which was creating a vacuum – an unbeknown or subconscious vacuum of force directed towards him – had been reversed, and in this reversal of energy he had become radiant.

5. Insects in Japan

Respect gets results even in subtle creatures like insects. On my first night in Tokyo for the centenary celebrations of Judo, I noticed an enormous spider on the wall of the guest room in which I and fourteen other Judo students were to sleep. Not knowing the customs and methods for handling these seemingly delicate species, I asked my senior teacher what to do, and what was the most appropriate way of approaching the hostess. My teacher walked in to examine the size of the spider, then produced no further comfort in me when she said in her mild Japanese voice, 'Oh, that kind, when that one bites it makes your face swell to three times its size *or* you die.' So she took the initiative and informed our hostess who, after examining the formidable creature, called in her two sons to deal with the situation. I will never forget it. The first thing one of them did was to open the sliding glass door to which the spider turned its head, as though it was reading the man's signal. Meanwhile, the other son brought in a teacup and chopsticks. He then gently touched the spider which seemed telepathically to understand and crawled willingly into the teacup with its legs dangling over the rim. He carried the royal spider to the door, knelt down and allowed it to crawl outside to freedom. I was impressed. From then on I watched the insects in Japan and noticed that they all seemed to have a heightened sensitivity about them. I found out later when discussing this at a dinner party that the Japanese are influenced by the religion of Shintoism which reveres ancestors and nature-spirits. The insects are treated with respect as they may be a deceased ancestor. It was evident to me that this respect was reflected back via the intelligence and responsiveness of the insects.

6. The Corkscrew Willow Waltz

Everything Has an Essence, a Voice, an Intelligence
One evening, I was preaching the above message to my class. Afterwards a student presented me with a bouquet of corkscrew willow branches. I was so taken by their beauty that I sat down that

very night and composed a ballad to the branches and named it the *Corkscrew Willow Waltz*. So different was the style of this music from my usual composition, with its many twists and turns and modulations, that I concluded, as did others, that I must have been a scribe to the voice of the branches.

The heart is the centre through which we relate in the Fountain. The mind is the expressor. In the exchange of information, giving and taking, listening and contributing, a circuit of vital energy is created – one composed of the balance of the yin and yang forces.

Who you are is a reflection of my heart. And in all that I see is the truth that's living inside of me.

S. MATTHEWS SCOTT

The Use of the Fountain

Not only will the Fountain organize your consciousness for greater ease in relating, it also allows you to derive more from relationships, strengthens your heart and the sense of being connected with the Earth, its inhabitants and nature.

Sometimes people don't always say what they mean. Likewise, we don't always say what we mean. We can use the Fountain to gain greater insight into the contents of people's hearts and improve our understanding of others as a result. We can also use the Fountain mode to increase our understanding of our motives, our drives, or, in Brechtian terms, the essential force behind all our interactions.

In the modern martial art of Aikido one learns to diffuse useless conflict by literally taking the other person's perspective. The ideology is of a win-win nature. On a mental level the one being attacked seizes the conflict as fuel for his or her strength. Anything that opposes one becomes a potential source of power for the Aikido practitioner. The effect of this attitude is that the one attacking is drained of the aggression and directed to the natural conclusion of their action. This may result in the attacker 'hurting themselves' as the flowing one or defender redirects the attack back to the aggressor. The higher one progresses in the art of Aikido, the quicker the recognition of the seeds of potential aggression and thus the quicker and more subtle the diffusion. The application can be seen when two people are having an argument. The moment one takes the position of the other the conflict is resolved. *The most difficult thing for some of us is letting go of the need to be right and, consequently, for the other to be wrong.*

In Fountain mode there is room for many perspectives. In fact one can look at a fountain as an expression of numerous perspectives, many energies asserting themselves harmoniously. In the Taoist saying: 'Many spokes unite to form the wheel but it is the centre which makes them useful. It is the centre which sets them into motion.' So it follows in a group situation that the one who can access the intention of each perspective and organize them all into a useful situation is the most centred, and emerges with an enriched perspective. **The more inclusive the perspective, the more choice that person has, and therefore the more personal power.** Such is the case when one plays or listens to Bach. The counterpoint, or harmonious combination of simultaneous parts or voices for which he is so famous, is a perfect illustration of enlightened community living. All for one and one for all is the theory in practice here. To live thus one must be living from the heart, since it is at heart level that a sense of abundance and balance is possible.

Humanity is in a state of evolution from the competitive, exclusive and greed state of consciousness to that of the heart. This is the major reason for the apparent increase in sudden disasters and worldwide environmental problems. We are being shaken up on a massive scale so that we can begin to feel the pain we are causing others as well as ourselves with our competitive attitudes. We are being offered the chance to change and grow. This is a great stretch for most of us. The other reason for the increase in disasters is as a result of the cause and effect cycle or karma we have incurred by our abuse of the Earth and her natural resources. This is not to say that progress is a bad thing. Rather that as we progress in our inventions and conveniences, we must be aware of the spirit in which we use the natural resource and the effect we cause in so doing.

Use the Fountain as a tool for integrating the many voices conflicting or not within yourself. Use it to balance your active and receptive natures – the yin and yang in you. Enjoy the moment. Listen to your gut feelings. Let your words come from your heart more and more. Beyond the content listen to the *intent* of what others are saying. Move instinctively. Trust that there is abundance. There is enough for everyone. There is enough for you. Bring the chalice of your heart to be filled by those who are expressing their talents, those whose example and work is life-supporting and inspirational. Bring it to be filled by the beauty and ways of nature such as flowing with the seasons and allowing your ideas to unfold stage by stage, from seed to full blossom. Learn to recognize which state your idea or project is in and hold your ground rather than comparing yourself with others. Allow your creativity to flow freely through you. Remember your heritage. This is the purpose of the Fountain.

The Fountain mode brings strength to our uniqueness by revealing more of our character as we interact spontaneously from our hearts. We learn about ourselves through the way we relate to others, as the Zen saying goes.

THE SHOWER OF LIGHT

The Shower of Light is particularly designed for those of us in the teaching, healing and performing professions because it is about spreading inspiration to humanity.

Practising the Shower of Light Physically

1. Assume the stance as for the Pump and Fountain. The Shower of Light is the reverse of the Fountain.

Figure 8 The Shower of Light

CHI KUNG: RECLAIM YOUR POWER

2. Imagine a shower of light filling your body from head to toes.

3. With your forearms and hands at your sides, turn your palms up and continue the motion up towards your head. Keep your elbows slightly below shoulder level for this part.

4. Once the hands are six inches from your head press downwards just in front of your body to just below your hips. Now begin the exercise again. Do this nine times initially, then build up gradually to eighteen.

The Meaning and Use of the Shower of Light

The purpose of the Shower of Light is to prepare and tune the body for the wattage of energy required to communicate in a meaningful way to a large group of people. The energy of the shower is much softer and lighter in its texture than the previous two Chi cybernetic modes. It comes down through the mind and body like a luminous mist bringing insight, information, ideas about moving on, answers to mysteries. Just as the morning mist nourishes an entire city, the shower's purpose is to nourish the greatest area and the greatest number. Any activity that disseminates information of an inspirational nature on a massive scale belongs to this category of Chi cybernetics. Publishing is a shower of light activity as are concerts, films, media and other forms of sharing one's gospel with the world. The function of these media is to educate, inspire and expand the individual's awareness beyond the mundane affairs of life. The more open one becomes energetically in the shower mode, the greater the ability to transmit to increasingly greater spheres of influence.

Having mastered the Fountain mode, one may use the Shower of Light to share something which has been discovered, that is uplifting to humanity. This process begins with self-realization, with seeking universal qualities internally. In a way, one becomes a conscious scientist whilst in the shower mode: action research is the means by which these discoveries are realized. This is the nature of the teacher – one whose fountain is spilling over the boundaries of one to one communication. Once discovered, lived and proven, the teacher is compelled to share the treasure she or he has unveiled to a larger number.

In view of the unprecedented aura that surrounds such a finding, shyness and fear may be the first emotions one feels as this new information comes through. This is a natural first stage in the shower mode for it is in the discovery of our uniqueness that we have the greatest fear and the greatest power. Once we acknowledge that this is happening we may use the other function of the shower which is to refine. The more finely tuned the heart, the more one can go beyond listening to the contents of another's heart, to listening to the deeper, approaching trends of the political climate, and to the social response. One becomes sensitive to the pulse of humanity at its most universal level. One's ability to interpret information in a practical, meaningful way improves. One becomes a voice for the people.

In Shower of Light mode ask yourself:

1. How can I open my head, my heart and guts to receive illumination to grow?
2. What is this illumination telling me?

THE PEBBLE IN THE LAKE

The Pebble in the Lake is designed to fan the flame of confidence and creativity. It is particularly geared to the artist, the entrepreneur, and all who wish to expand their creative instincts out into the world. Just as the name implies, the Pebble in the Lake urges us to promote our skills and crafts into increasingly large arenas. It can be utilized to push boundaries, to see how, for instance, science and philosophy and Eastern and Western thinking intersect. Any time we take our simple ideas into full bloom we are practising the Pebble in the Lake power.

MILLIE, A WISE FURRY WHISKERED ONE AMONG THEM

She watched me limp from the bottom of the stairs up to the landing. This injury to my hip was perhaps the most painful experience I had ever encountered. A trip to the toilet was an expedition which took half an hour to forty minutes mental preparation, since merely standing was a major feat. This particular trip up to the next floor was especially difficult. She waited patiently in all her whiskered feline splendour until I had made it to the top of what felt like something beyond Mount Everest before she delivered her quiet sermon. There I was perspiring, catching my breath, and feeling a bit sorry for myself when she began limping up the stairs, mimicking me with excruciating precision. She took her time and was careful to give each step the equal opportunity of her exaggerated limp. When she arrived I was hurt. I asked how dare she imitate me like that when I was in such pain. She just stood there staring at me and after a few moments I realized this was not a person I was quarrelsome with – it was a 17-year-old cat. This realization made me laugh hysterically for nearly an hour. As soon as I started laughing she looked pleased with herself. Mission accomplished.

Practising the Pebble in the Lake Physically

1. Assume the stance of the previous exercises.

2. Begin by bringing your hands into a parallel position just in front of your lower abdomen.

3. Now reach forward with your arms, leading with the tips of your middle fingers, whilst maintaining the parallel position.

4. Next feel into the blades of your hands and expand them towards the sides, in front of your body.

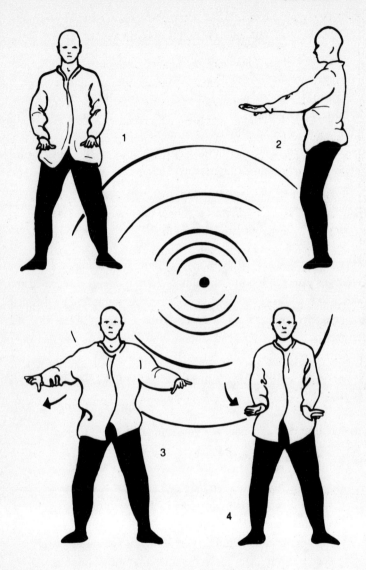

Figure 9 The Pebble in the Lake

5. Finally, concentrate on the insides of your hands and wrists and draw your hands back into their original position. Do this nine times, then build up gradually to eighteen.

As you do the Pebble in the Lake feel the energy expanding all around you, as though you are the pebble and the energy is creating continuously emanating concentric circles. Feel this expansion at the back of you as well as at the front. Feel how you are opening the space around you, making more room for your heart and dreams to be realized.

The Meaning of the Pebble in the Lake

When given space to grow, water and nourishment the seed emerges into full bloom over time. When we have integrated the other four Chi cybernetic ways of being, we live as freely blooming flowers, always reseeding ourselves. There is a sense of eternity. The concentric circles appear to stop at the shore line, but in fact their energy impulse carries on and on. We have merely to set it in motion and remain in the centre of the flow. 'Don't push the river', is the phrase used in Chi Kung practice.

In Pebble in the Lake mode ask yourself:

1. What does expansion mean to me?
2. How have I already expanded this week?
3. Where and what is the boundary to this expansion?
4. Do you see the end? If so, where?
5. If you are the eldest child in your family can you see yourself exceeding your father's expression in the world and your mother's in the home? (Remember: a mark of good parents and teachers is that their children and students go beyond them in some way.)

THE MOUNTAIN

Keeping still. Recognizing what one has and building upon it, standing one's ground in the face of opposition is the purpose of the Mountain. The sense of the Mountain can be heard in the words of the following Native American chant:

Where I stand is holy
Holy is the ground
Forest, mountain, river . . . listen to the sound.
Great Spirits circle all around me.

Practising the Mountain Physically

1. Take the usual stance.
2. Make your arms round and stretched as though they were encircling the globe.
3. As your hands come together form a triangle with them and press through the blades of your hands. Stand like a mountain. Feel yourself as one. Do this nine times. Then build up to eighteen.

The Meaning and Use of the Mountain

We build directional strength by taking one step at a time, making sure that at each stage we are mentally, physically and emotionally integrated, as well as being secure and integrated into society whilst retaining our individuality. The Mountain relates to the innocence of the child within and will power of our elders.

Age as Strength

Play as Children as a Source of Fulfilment
The way we played as a child contains all the clues for ways of being and vocational interests that are fulfilling. Remember how you

Figure 10 The Mountain

played when you were having the best time. This included reading, use of the imagination and playing on one's own. Meditate on the details in your play and see how many of those, symbolic or literal, are alive in you now. Which ones have been left out? How do you intend to reclaim and incorporate them?

The Strength of the Elders

The will to have lived for many years, to have weathered life's storms and obstacles, and life's transitions produces a strength that one cannot have in youth. I have seen this demonstrated time after time when teaching the unbendable arm exercise to those over 60. They usually feel that they shouldn't try because they are not strong enough. Once I coax them to have a go, we are all amazed at the amount of inner strength they have, even in wheelchairs. In recognizing this strength one grandmother said, 'If more of the elderly were on the streets at night, violence would be non-existent.' I'm inclined to agree with her. This is what the Mountain is about – about clinging to our heritage, about trusting our own timing, about appreciating all that we have survived.

Mountain Attitude; Crises = Opportunities

This is the belief in the martial arts of Chi Kung, Aikido and Kung-fu. Every obstacle is an opportunity to grow. It doesn't mean that we don't feel discomfort in the midst of change. It refers initially to the way we frame an experience in retrospect and, increasingly, the way we approach difficult times. In the television series *Stand Your Ground* one pupil reflected upon her rape experience as a chance to confront all her fears rather than as a withering victim. We talked about her as a rape survivor which she described as 'changing the ideological context', putting her into a position of power and the rapist as a coward.

Two weeks before the deadline of this book, I lost two years' work when another computer failed and wiped it clean. Nearly devastated, I was asked to take a big dose of what I preach. I took this as an opportunity to distil my thoughts further and to upgrade my

CHI KUNG: RECLAIM YOUR POWER

equipment. Every time we reflect on how we survived unpleasant situations, on how they could have been much worse, we learn the lessons and move on. We are practising Mountain mode.

Commitment and Discipline
When we learn a skill thoroughly, when we follow through with commitment, when we build friendships, businesses, love on a solid foundation, we are in Mountain mode.

In Mountain mode ask yourself:

1. Under what circumstances do I lose my timing?
2. What gives me strength? Which types of strength get me lasting results?

The wind was now her friend. It always brought tidings of new opportunities – an exalting adventure of new parts of self to be revealed and explored, for now the wind had become a symbol of change – always an exceptional chance to grow. In a way, it had become the very breath of life.

6

TAPPING ESSENCE POWER IN YOUR STAR SIGN

AFFIRMATIONS AND EXERCISES FOR CENTRING

The purpose of the following astrological section is not to freeze each of us into a convenient category or to provide an excuse for our actions, rather it is meant to be a catalyst and a supplement in our appreciation of our unique gifts and those of others.

In the realm of expanded awareness each of us chooses the time, date and place of our birth. Each season with its varying nuances expresses a particular point of view: each is necessary for understanding the whole picture of our interaction with universal forces. All points of view are within us, and some are stronger than others. Astrology is one of the oldest sciences. When used properly it can guide us with a compassionate language – one which speaks to uniqueness.

Again, all the star signs are within each of us in a particular area of life. Those of you who are familiar with your birth chart may find where the following affirmations and Chi cybernetic exercises are relevant for you. As for the rest of us, know that the symbol for the star sign is the circle with the dot in the centre ☉. This refers both to the astronomical constellation and to the sense of purpose in which you feel centred, your place in the universe. So, at the end of the day, it is in the meaning of our star sign where we find centring. Further understanding will come when you locate the exact area of life of your star sign.

When practised regularly and with relaxed intent the Chi cybernetic exercises will empower your body to reinforce your sense of purpose.

ARIES

You teach us the art of assertiveness to 'boldly go where none has gone before'. Your impulsive nature is the key to our individual freedom.

Recommended Chi Cybernetic Exercises
Do the mental/physical Pebble in the Lake exercise to empower your communion with the source of your impulses – weekly, preferably on Tuesday mornings for the first month, then on the day and time of your choice from then on.

TAURUS

You remind us of the simple ways we may bring heaven to earth. You show us how to enjoy our bodies and to love the comforts of the earth. You teach us the importance of giving back to the earth.

Recommended Chi Cybernetic Exercises
1. Do the Pump to prevent inertia, three times a week.
2. Do the Mountain to strengthen your values and your sense of quality.

Gemini

You remind us of our personal genius. You show us the way of versatility and teach us the beauty of keeping light and witty. You demonstrate the power of having many interpretations.

Recommended Chi Cybernetic Exercises
1. Do the Fountain daily to keep your body and perceptions fresh and sensitive to others.
2. Do the Shower of Light daily to keep in tune with your intuitive nature.
3. Do the Pebble in the Lake daily to strengthen the depth of your information banks.

Cancer

You remind us of the hidden river of life in our feelings. You show us how the child inside can make the garden of our dreams come true.

Recommended Chi Cybernetic Exercises
1. Do the Pump to build the memory of emotional security in volatile conditions, on the new and full moons (day or night and preferably near a lake or in a garden).
2. Do the Pebble in the Lake to clarify memories of inner treasures, also on the new and full moons.

LEO

You break the rules and teach us the importance of humour and spontaneous self-expression. You remind us to follow the adventure of our instincts, to love, and live from our hearts. After all, life is just one big play!

Recommended Chi Cybernetic Exercises
1. Do the Fountain to stimulate your heart, whenever you feel like it.
2. Do the Mountain to strengthen your radiance, whenever you feel in the mood.

VIRGO

You nurture self-improvement. Selfless service is your vehicle. You find asylum in nature. Ironically, you are the keeper of the spirit because you make sure all the parts are working efficiently.

Recommended Chi Cybernetic Exercises
1. Do the Pump to stimulate the overall efficient flow of energy through your body and brain, at the beginning and at the end of the week (preferably outside in nature).
2. Do the Shower to relax the intestines and to release any repression or feelings of guilt, at the beginning and at the end of the week. Do this just before your first meal of the day.

LIBRA

You create beauty and harmony. You bridge the gap between the spiritual and material worlds. When you realise the equal importance of both you step off the fence of indecision.

Recommended Chi Cybernetic Exercises
1. Do the Pump to balance the yin and yang forces inside – once a month in the morning upon waking (preferably in a beautiful setting).
2. Do the Shower of Light to keep your mind illuminated – once a month in the morning upon waking (in a beautiful setting).
3. Do the Mountain to strengthen your grounding and ingenuity in the material world – fortnightly, before going to bed (preferably outside under the night sky).

SCORPIO

Your natural instinct is to go against the grain of merely living in the shadows. You emerge from the deep waters of life. You remind us to tap the underlying essence in everything. You reveal to us the mystery of life, death and the beyond.

Recommended Chi Cybernetic Exercise
1. Do the Pump on the new moon to relax you in your persuasive and transformative abilities.

SAGITTARIUS

You inspire us to reach higher. You bring us perspective and confidence. You see clearly with the inner eye.

Recommended Chi Cybernetic Exercises
1. Do the Fountain to replenish your ever-flowing enthusiasm, any time on Thursdays (preferably after mentally visualizing your favourite foreign countryside).
2. Do the Shower of Light to keep you in touch with the source of your intuition – any time you wish.
3. Do the Pebble in the Lake to keep you in touch with your confidence to share inspirational information and to keep the space clear around you – daily.

CAPRICORN

You are an organizer at the highest level in the greatest spheres of influence. You build your empire one brick at a time. You naturally know how to do this. When you soar with the eagles you are never lonely, even in your darkest hour. Remember your spiritual heritage. Realize who you are.

Recommended Chi Cybernetic Exercises
1. Do the Mountain to confirm your stamina and concentration – three times a day for the first month, then once a week for the second month, and once a month on the full moon for the third month (preferably in majestic settings).

2. Do the Fountain to keep you in touch with your heritage, one Saturday each season of the year.
3. Do the Pebble in the Lake to remind you to delegate responsibility – once a week on Sundays.

AQUARIUS

You refresh tradition with new ways of the future. You teach us that stereotyping is the mother of invention. You remind us that 'All for one and one for all' is the window to truth.

Recommended Chi Cybernetic Exercise
Do the Shower of Light to keep you in touch with the vision of the future, once in a while.

PISCES

You move to the music of humanity's deepest need. You know the coming trends. You show us compassion for the people who are cast into institutions and other forms of our social plumbing. You heal the rifts between all our differences.

Recommended Chi Cybernetic Exercises
1. Do the Shower of Light to keep your finger on the misty pulse of life – twice weekly on Tuesday and Wednesday evenings before retiring.
2. Do the Pebble in the Lake to strengthen your presence in lateral thinking – twice weekly upon waking on Tuesday and Wednesday mornings.

THE TEACHER AMONG THEM

PEONY, THE BLOSSOM IN THE SPRING

And when asked the secret of its lovely immortal existence, it spoke peacefully and suggested the following progression of affirmations:

1. *All the seeds of who I am are in the warmth of my belly. All are expressed through the depths of my heart.* (**The Seed**)

2. *I warm these seeds daily as I move instinctively.* (**Gestation**)

3. *I allow my ideas to be tested at the appropriate stage with joy. My roots become stronger.* (**The Roots**)

4. *I respond to the call to demonstrate in the world that which I believe.* (**The Stem**)

5. *I enrich my experiences as I share them with others.* (**The Leaves**)

6. *I recognize when my ideas are about to bear fruit – to blossom. I prepare for the harvest.* (**Waiting** and **Trusting**)

7. *I deepen and mature the fruit by allowing it to become fertilized by the night in the darkest hours. When everything appears to close down, to go wrong, I take this as a sign that I am about to grow . . . my ideas are in their final testing grounds before they blossom. I wait for the blossom.* (**The Opening** and **Apparent Close** of the **Bud** before it goes to full bloom)

8. *I open gracefully to the highest levels of revelation for my level of understanding.* (**The Blooming**)

9. *I return to the source of my ideas and find that it has expanded.* (**The Dropping** of the **Petals, the Composting**)

10. *I celebrate the giving and receiving impulses of my source.* (**Propagating, Naturalizing**)

11. *I practise detachment without cruelty. I welcome each stage of learning:*

a. In the Mist – *information and meaning seem interesting but still misty.*

b. In the Water – *information feels familiar in the body.*

c. In the Light – *information has been integrated and mastered. One observes oneself performing.*

> Stages of learning referred to
> by Capoeira Master Bira, from
> the Afro-Brazilian martial art

RECLAIMING OUR POWER

THE LANDMARKS

Here are some landmarks to bear testimony to the fact that we are *understand*ing our power:

Introductory Statements

1. The statements 'I will, I won't, I choose to do it this way, and I didn't' replace the I shoulds, I shouldn't, and I should haves.

Standing Ground

2. We trust our instincts (not only our heads and calculations). We do not allow others to talk us out of our feelings of anger, sadness, joy, etc.

3. We are not intimidated by others' opinions unless they know us well and their opinions have been specifically requested. We do not listen to what others say we should do unless they have walked our path and/or truly they have direct experience in what they are recommending.

Our Bodies and Doctors

4. We actively love our bodies and participate in preventive health care activities. We train ourselves to listen to danger signals in our bodies and when called for, apart from a life or death emergency situation, we seek the diagnosis of at least three physicians before having major surgery.

Admitting Strengths and Limitations

5. We know what we are capable of doing ourselves and, equally when we need help.

6. We recognize and cease to be threatened by others who have the need to be verbally, or otherwise, aggressive, abusive, and to project their inadequacy on to us.

Quality Relationships

7. We choose friends, lovers and partners who love us for who we are rather than those who wish to shape us into their moulds.

> *The beginning of love is to let those we love be perfectly themselves, and not to twist them to fit our image. Otherwise we love only the reflection of ourselves we find in them.*
>
> THOMAS MERTON, *NO MAN IS AN ISLAND*

8. We love others for who they are rather than trying to make them dependent on us. We love from wholeness rather than to fill emptiness in ourselves. We love others for their wholeness rather than to save them or complete them.

Moving on from Fear and Ignorance

9. We recognize prejudice in ourselves and others as a product of fear and ignorance.

Waking Up

10. We find ourselves waking up earlier than usual, more relaxed, joyful and excited about the adventure of the day.

No Time Like the Present

11. We recognize and celebrate any discovery of a mental, physical or emotional block as a gift and opportunity to grow. Rather than continuously delving into whose fault it is, such as parents, old lovers, etc. (we could spend lifetimes digging up causes, and one will just lead to another), we ask ourselves: 'How am I going to deal with it *right now?*'

Being in Tune

12. Coincidences or synchonistic events occur more frequently. We do not relegate our intuitive and waking up powers to the supernatural, the weird and the mystical.

Giving to Others

13. We realize that by loving ourselves we are improving the quality of what we give to others.

Nature as Teacher

14. We increasingly appreciate the beauty and intelligence of nature as well as our abilities to improve technology.

Listening

15. We can listen to the intent of others because we understand our own motives.

True Strength

16. We move more gracefully through crises and painful experiences. We learn from them. We recognize how we have *survived and become stronger* and learn from these experiences.

Embracing our Heritage

17. We allow the **chi**ld inside to play.

18. We open to the beauty of our heritage.

Physical/Mental Development

19. We use our minds to become more inclusive of all facets of life.

20. We use our minds, our feelings and our bodies to discriminate the 'wheat from the chaff'.

Replacing Envy

21. We recognize the greatness in others and therefore in ourselves.

22. We realize there is room for all our unique expressions in the world. We realize that change begins within ourselves, first and foremost.

I have seen so many people come to life, into being who they want to be, after they have been diagnosed as terminally ill. Though I celebrate this awakening, I also appreciate that they are reminding us that we can do this earlier in our lives. I appreciate the message that dis-ease has to do with going away from ourselves to please others.

HAPPINESS RUNS

Happiness runs in a circular motion,
We are all like little ships upon the sea,
All our thoughts are deeper than we can see,
We can have it all if we let ourselves be.

Everything is a part of everything anyway,
We can have it all if we let ourselves be.
Happiness runs. Happiness runs . . .

(A Song I learned. Many thanks to the composer who is unknown.)

LANDSCAPING PERSONAL POWER

Daily Affirmations for Earth Angels

Repeat aloud three times each and every morning upon waking. Be aware of how you have done each of these acts at the end of every day. This will become your artist palette and will encourage you to reclaim your power. To enhance the strength of the affirmations, touch each of the places in brackets with your middle right finger whilst reciting.

1. I see the whole picture; I act with wisdom. (crown)
2. I see clearly through all appearances. (between eyebrows)
3. I experience the beauty in life. (nose, eyes, ears and tongue)
4. I express myself clearly. All that fulfils me comes to me. (throat)
5. I open with joy to receive and give love. I express courage and compassion. (centre of chest)

6. I move through all obstacles. I meet all challenges with strength and will power. (solar plexus)
7. I live from the wellspring of my dreams. (navel)
8. I experience pleasure in all I do. My creativity is unlimited. (middle of public bone)
9. I climb with ease to the top of my goals. (knee)
10. I am connected to the earth. I give back to the earth. (soles of feet and big toes)

Epilogue

More and more of us are waking up every day.
As it is written so we are living it . . .

Kaleghl lives and teaches in London, in Europe and in the United States. For further information about courses related to the book write:

Kaleghl Quinn's Life Force Arts
2 West Heath Drive
London NW11

Reclaim Your Power Empowering Cards are available from the above address.